ECCE HOMO

PRODUCTION
EDITA-LAUSANNE

Library of Congress catalog card number: 62-17084

Joseph Jobé

ECCE HOMO

Harper & Row Publishers　　　　New York and Evanston

AUTHOR'S PREFACE

As the result of a decree by Caesar Augustus, Mary and Joseph had to go to Bethlehem to register themselves. They spent the night in a stable, where Mary gave birth to Jesus Christ, whom she laid in a manger. On that most precious of all nights a Saviour came down from Heaven into an unheeding and unsuspecting world. On that night, too, Mary and Joseph, the first to worship the Christ, watched over His cradle: they were followed by the shepherds, and later by the Magi. And since that night an ever growing number of Christians have followed, often through blood and tears, pressing on in hope towards His and their Father's home.

In the course of centuries the Gospel has been preached in every continent and to all nations. Today Christians are numbered in hundreds of millions and, in spite of the different denominations which exist, they are united in a common faith in their Redeemer.

It is well known that from the earliest times Christians have wished to portray, either in painting or sculpture, the features of their Redeemer, also that such portrayal has not been and even now is not universally approved. But simple people need visible expression to support their piety, and in all periods of Christian history the different peoples and races of the world have developed their own styles and modes in which to express their common faith.

In Imperial Rome Christians borrowed from the traditions of the pagan arts. Byzantine influence affected all the Mediterranean basin, and examples are found in Coptic, Orthodox and Roman Catholic Churches in the West. Gothic art flourished in our cathedrals in an incomparable burst of mystic beauty. With all its rich diversity the Renaissance resulted in a certain insipidity of religious feeling. Today Christianity is not restricted to the shores of the Mediterranean, nor Christian art to that of Europe or the Near East. From all Christian peoples, of whatever race, country or continent, there now bursts forth—like a choir whose different voices merge in a harmonious whole—a new Christian art, diverse in its forms of expression, universal in being inspired by one faith. The Christ of all the world.

The West knew Him in the Middle Ages, when the church was also the people's home. From the time of the Renaissance Christian art split up. On the one hand religious art developed along the lines and according to the canons of the national arts, Italian, Flemish, Spanish or French painting. Today's art seeks to recover the magic power of Christian symbols in a less figurative style.

On the other hand the art of the people, an inheritance from the Middle Ages, developed alongside the grand art, reviving with difficulty and often going astray. Now that an ever spreading industrialism threatens the art of these image makers, people are discovering in them many qualities before despised. Statues, ceramics and small paintings on glass, the creation of numberless devoted Christians, though often awkward and un-couth in their rustic simplicity, testify to the piety of bygone generations, and stir the emotions of contempo-rary man. And today, in this twentieth century, those missionary countries now on the way to independence enrich Christian iconography by using their own traditions and styles to portray the truths of the world-wide Gospel.

In Asia Christian sculptures and pictures are influenced by the ancient traditions of the arts of India, China and Japan, and even by Buddhist themes, just as the earliest Christians were influenced by the old Roman tradition. Africa, whose traditions are often obscure and somewhat materialistic, expresses its naive soul with restrained sim-plicity. Here are records from every part of the world, drawn from every epoch and in the most diverse styles and techniques: but they are those of simple people, little known or anonymous. They will give Christians the world over an opportunity of discovering and comparing them, but especially of becoming aware, beyond the forms and techniques, of the great spirit of brotherhood uniting them with their brothers in God to form the great family of Man.

INTRODUCTION

There is an astonishing element about Christ's earthly life. It had been foretold by the Prophets, and the Evangelists have left an account of it, but yet we have no certain knowledge of the date either of His birth or of His death.

The title "Christ", by which He is generally known, is, of course, the Greek name Χριστός, a literal translation of the Hebrew, "Messiah", which means "the Anointed One", or "the Lord's Anointed". But there survives no record of His features, either pictorial or descriptive. The Evangelists record His teaching, but whether He was tall or short, what were His physique and colouring, what the intonation of His voice when speaking to Mary Magdalene or cleansing the Temple of the money-changers, of all these details we are left in ignorance. On the other hand no life has so profoundly affected the human race and human affairs as that of the Son of Man, who was born in a stable and who died upon a cross. For the rule of law and revenge He substituted that of love and forgiveness.

Throughout the ages faithful Christians have carried this Gospel to the furthest corners of the world, and preached it to all nations in every country. And in all ages men have felt the need to create some picture of the Saviour's features, if only as an encouragement to them in this "vale of tears". How, then, have men sought to represent Christ's features?

SYMBOLS AND SYMBOLIC PICTURES OF CHRIST

The question can be answered only by considering the earliest pictures.

The early Church did not seek any pictorial representation of Christ's features, but was content to recall them by means of symbols which, though clear enough to the initiated, were sufficiently obscure or insignificant to allay the suspicions of their pagan rulers. These symbols are still in use. First there is the monogram, or chrism of Christ. This consists of the first two letters of the Greek word Χριστός, viz. X and P, which are interlaced. Since the fourteenth century there exists also a Latin equivalent in the letters I. H. S. which are variously interpreted. One interpretation reads it as "Jesus Hominum Salvator", i.e. "Jesus, Saviour of Men"; another reads it as "In Hoc Signo (vinces)", i.e. "In this sign (ye shall conquer.)"

Another symbol was that of the fish, either painted or sculpted. According to St. Augustine it symbolised the descent of Christ into the depths of the human condition, just as the fish descends unharmed to the bottom of the sea. But the more literal interpretation is really preferable. The Greek word for fish is ΙΧΘΥΣ, which gives the acrostic Ἰησοῦς Χριστός, Θεοῦ Υἱός, Σωτήρ (Jesus Christ, Son of God, Saviour).

Another symbol borrowed from animal life was the lamb. It is based on many passages from the Bible, both Old and New Testaments, e.g. Isaiah 53 : 7, and Revelation 5 : 6. From the seventh century this symbol gradually disappeared from a large part of Christendom.

In A.D. 692 the Quinisext Council,[1] held at Constantinople, ordered that in future Christ must be pictured as a human being, and not under the symbol of a lamb.

"Having formerly allowed these figures as symbols and emblems, today we give first place to grace and truth, that is the fullness of faith. Therefore that all may look upon His perfection, even through the medium of painting, we decree that in future the Lord Christ must be pictured as a man instead of as a lamb, so that we may contemplate the sublime humility of the Word made flesh. The artist must lead us in memory to see Jesus living, suffering and dying for our salvation and the redemption of the world."

This prohibition seems to have affected chiefly the Eastern Church: in central and western Europe the theme of the Lamb of God was retained, but used less than the human representation of Christ. But in the Lateran Museum and in the catacombs can be seen figures of Christ as a man—the Good Shepherd, the Fisher of Souls. The early Christians did not regard these as actual portraits, but as symbolic representations of Christ. The basis was the Scriptures, though the form was borrowed from Greek and Roman statuary, e.g. Orpheus, Hermes Kriophoros, etc. An excellent example of this is the theme of the Good Shepherd, based as it is on both the Old and New Testaments, e.g. Psalm 23, Ezekiel 34 : 12, Isaiah 40 : 11, and Luke 15 : 3-7, John 10 : 1-16, as well as on the pagan prototype of Hermes Kriophoros. It is Christ, the Good Shepherd who, seeking the salvation of sinners, goes after them and brings them back, repentant, into the bosom of the flock. In His physical aspect He is just a Greek or Roman shepherd, usually a beardless adolescent, with curly hair, and holding a shepherd's crook, or even a Pan-pipe. The well-known statuette in the Lateran Museum showing the Good Shepherd carrying a lamb on his shoulders is a typical example of this most popular type. This symbolism has survived, being found in modern art and popular image-making. It must not, of course, be confused with pictures of John the Baptist, who is often depicted accompanied by a lamb.

---

[1] Also, and generally known as the Trullan Synod. The Western Church does not recognise it as ecumenical.

SUPPOSED PORTRAITS OF CHRIST

After the lapse of several centuries Christians, now freed from fear of persecution and encouraged by the Church, were able openly to venerate the portrait of their Saviour. It was not so long after the actual events that there might not be some chance of consulting, even of finding, a design or picture which had been preserved by the piety of the faithful. The Scriptures contained no authentic description, but there might exist some verbal tradition handed down through succeeding generations: possibly even relics dating from the time of Jesus.

Chronologically the earliest supposed picture of Christ is said to have come into existence during His lifetime, but there exists neither scriptural nor historical basis for the story: its first mention is not before the beginning of the fourth century. It is reported in varying forms by Eusebius (c. 260-c. 340) and in the Doctrine of Addai (c. 400). A fairly full account appears in a passage from the Golden Legend of Jacob de Voragine (middle of thirteenth century), of which the following is a résumé. Abgar, King of Edessa, wrote to Jesus inviting Him to come to stay so as to escape the malice of His fellow Jews. Jesus refused the invitation and Abgar then sent to Him an artist commissioned to paint His portrait. The artist was so overcome by the radiance of Christ's face, that he became unable to paint: whereupon Jesus placed the artist's cloak against His face, leaving on it the impression of His features. This was brought to Abgar after the Ascension by the apostles Simon and Jude. After various vicissitudes the portrait is said now to be in the Church of San Silvestro in Capite in Rome. Of the portrait—authentic or not—there are several derivatives, i.e. the Holy Face of Laon, the carved mask in the Cathedral of Ioureiev-Polki, and many others to be found in Byzantine, Russian and Serbian Churches. Another supposed portrait of Our Lord is the imprint left by Him on Veronica's headcloth. According to the legend, a woman named Veronica offered her headcloth to Our Lord to wipe the blood and sweat from His face on the way to Calvary. To thank her for her pious act, Jesus restored it to her with His features impressed on it. This "Veronica's Veil" was said to be one of the well-known relics in St. Peter's, Rome, which disappeared at the sack of the city in A.D. 1527. This legend cannot with the least certainty be pronounced authentic: it appears in a Bible of Roger d'Argenteuil, but it must be remembered that Veronica is nowhere mentioned in Scripture, also that the name itself, vera εἰκων, etymologically means "true picture", so it is possible that the woman has taken existence from the cloth. Anyhow, there is no historical foundation for Abgar's picture or Veronica's headcloth.

There are other legendary portraits. The Evangelist Luke is supposed to have painted a portrait of Mary, the mother of Jesus, and he is also said to have begun one of Our Lord, which was miraculously finished by angels. The legend of Nicodemus tells of a similar miracle: long after the Ascension he tried to sculpt a crucifix from memory. While doing so he fell asleep, and on waking found the crucifix completed, with Christ's head carved on it. In the eighth century this crucifix got to Lucca, in Italy, and is said to be the one shown under a "tempietto", the work of Matteo Civitali (fifteenth century). Under the wrong name of St. Voult of Lucca it was a popular object of devotion during the last part of the Middle Ages, and there are many copies of it in France and Belgium.

But none of these supposed contemporary portraits has any real claim to authenticity, and it is safe to assume that they came into existence many centuries after Our Lord's earthly life. The conclusion is inescapable: as Irenaeus,

Bishop of Lyons wrote, "The physical features of Jesus are unknown to us"; and to the same effect Augustine of Hippo, "We are completely ignorant of what He looked like". And paradoxical as it appears, it is true, as Dom Leclercq writes:

"It is hardly possible that if Christ's earthly ministry had been in a Greek or Latin country, in Alexandria or Antioch, Ephesus, Athens or Rome, there would not have been left to us some iconographic memorial, either contemporary or nearly so." (*Dictionnaire d'Archéologie Chrétienne, vol. VII, 2. Art. Jésus-Christ, Col. 2394.*) But Christ's earthly ministry was wholly among a people who were suspicious of all attempts to depict the human body. To paint or sculpt a person's features was very liable to bring down an accusation of idolatry. Probably here lies the reason for the complete absence of any historical portrait of Our Lord. During the first two centuries of the Church's life symbolic figures alone were used: what the incarnate Jesus really looked like was of interest neither to artist nor theologian.

INVENTION OF AN ICONOGRAPHIC IDIOM

From the third century the Fathers of the Church began to wonder what, after all, Christ did look like. And in the fourth century appeared the first pictures which both the artists and the faithful believed to be accurate portraits of our Lord's features. But this Christ was not as we now see Him in Europe—a serene and kindly face, long wavy hair and beard, with strong lips and bright eyes. Some of the Fathers of the Church, on the authority of Isaiah 53 : 2, "he hath no form nor comeliness; and when we shall see him, there is no beauty that we should desire him", thought that our Lord had been an ugly man. The first of these, Justin Martyr (A.D. 100-c. 165) mentioned in his Dialogue with Tryppho, ch. 100, that the Son of God was a man "devoid of beauty and a sufferer". Tertullian (c. A.D. 160-c. 220) writes to the same effect, though more exaggeratedly: "There was nothing outstanding about Christ's flesh, and it was just this contrast with His personality which struck everyone ... far from emanating divine radiance His body had not even simple human beauty. Apart from the prophecy 'he hath no form nor comeliness', His passion and the humiliations He suffered left their mark. His body was seen to be truly human, deprived of all charm by His sufferings." Irenaeus (c. A.D. 130-c. 200), Origen (c. A.D. 185-c. 254) and Clement of Alexandria (c. A.D. 150-c. 215) held similar views.

Other doctors of the Church believed that Jesus was the best-looking of the children of men, on the authority of Psalm 45 : 3-4. "Thou art fairer than the children of men : full of grace are thy lips, because God hath blessed thee for ever. Gird thee with thy sword upon thy thigh, O thou most Mighty." Jerome (c. A.D. 342-420) writes : "All who saw Him were at once attracted by the divine brilliance which emanated from His person and lit up His countenance" (*in Mattheum, IX*). The same opinions were also held by Basil (c. A.D. 330-379), Chrysostom (c. A.D. 347-407) and Augustine (A.D. 354-430). The first opinion was the older one. The doctors—named above—who held it all died before A.D. 255 : also it is worth noticing that they all believed that Jesus wore a beard. The Fathers who held the second opinion were all born after the beginning of the fourth century and were influenced by the cultures of Greece and Rome. They probably had difficulty in envisaging the divine

as lacking beauty, and viewed with horror the idea of representing Christ as less beautiful than Apollo. As Apollo is always without a beard, so Christ is pictured beardless.

Early Christian art was influenced by these contradictory opinions, and for a long time one finds two separate types of portraiture:

(1) Of Syrian origin: this shows a bearded Christ majestic and virile, resembling an oriental monarch.

(2) Of Hellenistic origin: here Christ is shown clean-shaven; a handsome young adult, corresponding to the Greek ideal of an ephebe or young athlete. The mosaics at Ravenna and the Carolingian miniatures are good examples of these.

Whether or not Christ had been ugly, as Isaiah suggests, had ceased to be relevant: the artists, following the theologians, had decided that their representations of Christ must realize the perfection of human beauty. From the sixth century the art of the Christian East showed Christ exclusively as a majestic, long-bearded figure, while in the West both types persisted and the beardless Christ is found in most of the Carolingian miniatures and in the Roman art of the thirteenth century. From then on artists concentrated on showing some particular aspect of Christ's work. Thus the teaching Christ presents someone with a copy of the Gospel; the suffering Christ wears a crown of thorns; Christ the Judge of the World is represented with sceptre and orb, while Christ in triumph tramples underfoot all kinds of creeping things—the symbols of evil thoughts. He is recognized, too, by the halo, representing the radiance of His person. There has been an evolution in the manner of presenting Christ's person, with different types in different countries and also depending on the changes of religious thought and of civilizations. But all through there seems to be one fundamental principle which is accepted. "According to the Gospels, Christ always preserved His dignity, both among crowds and with His friends, as well as during the worst moments of His passion. It is therefore unworthy, indeed impious, to represent Christ's features as contemptible or repellent.

"Spiritually Jesus was the most perfect man. In spite of His omnipotence He was humble of heart, for did He not say 'I am among you as he that serveth'? Artists therefore have become imbued with the Gospel story in order that they may depict, in marble or wood, on parchment or paper, an authentic Christ, not necessarily materially but spiritually. What is important is not physical realism so much as to show the divine character illuminating the human framework."

The innumerable number of pictures painted by men of all races bears witness to the thousand different ways by which this purpose may be achieved.

THE CHRIST OF BYZANTIUM

In A.D. 476 the Roman Empire succumbed to the invader, and it was long before the West recovered from the troubled times that followed. In the meantime Byzantium, heir to the Greek and Syrian traditions, even to those of Sassanian Persia and Egypt, became patron of a new Christian art. Just as the first Christian artists had copied Greek heroes, so their Byzantine successors sought their inspiration in the pomp of the Byzantine Court. For many centuries two almost contradictory streams of Christian iconographic art stemmed from the Byzantine civilization. One type which became stereotyped was the hierarchical, seemingly out of this world and timeless. It depicted Christ as the Supreme King, Master of the World, the Creator, rising from a rainbow as from the beginning of time. This seemed to unite both Creator and Saviour in one person.

But a new fashion arose, especially after the tenth century, namely to use paintings to tell the story of Jesus' earthly ministry, thus making them more realistic.

And so alongside the sumptuous and statuesque art prevailing at the court, there grew up an independent monastic form, which expressed itself in the production of icons. Byzantine art gave occasion for disputes. The iconoclastic controversy—and many of the Emperors were iconoclasts—raged between A.D. 725 and 842. After the decision went against the iconoclasts, images were regarded as having something more than mere narrative or educational value, being in some way endowed with their subjects' mystical influences. They acquired a certain sacredness, and were closely associated with the liturgy. The holy images induced contemplation and encouraged action, for they represented Christ and invited the faithful to participate in His life. As Theodore of Studios writes, "The picture you see there is that of Christ; it is Christ Himself, at least in name. . . . Those who reverence it honour Christ; those who refuse to do so are His enemies." *(Quoted by Bréhin, L'Art chrétien.)*

Although to some extent supplanted by Western art from the eleventh or twelfth centuries, Byzantine iconography renewed and spread its influence in Eastern Europe, especially in Russia, Serbia, Bulgaria and Rumania, and even in Catholic Poland. Some of the monasteries, such as those on Mount Athos, preserved the old tradition of icons.

THE CHRIST IN THE ART OF WESTERN CHRISTENDOM

In the West, which was then emerging from disorder, there was about to be an expansion of the Roman and Gothic arts, giving men a new vision of Christ. At the start the Christian art of the West was again subject to Eastern influences. Thus from the Syrian tradition we get a bearded, from the Hellenistic a clean-shaven Christ. These parallel influences soon merged into a genuine Western style, the Gothic. An important feature during this long preparatory period was a controversy over images, similar to that in the East. This ended with the Council of Frankfurt (A.D. 794), which condemned the decree of the second Council of Nicaea (A.D. 787) on the worship of images.[1] Thereafter in the West images were treated as having only an educational value, a picture bible for the edification of the faithful. This new idea became fully developed in the art of the following centuries. The Roman period, still subject to Oriental influences, produced a new Christ—the Christ of the Apocalypse. Born in a climate of songs of valour, a heroic figure of superhuman proportions is set to welcome the faithful as they enter the church. On the basis of the more lurid Biblical texts, the Judge of the World is shown surrounded by devilish monsters, founding His kingdom on the annihilation of the universe and the punishment of sinners: a striking commentary on the text "the hour is coming, and now is, when the dead shall hear the voice of the Son of God; and they that hear shall live". *(John 5 : 25.)* Gothic art, largely inspired by theologians, brought clarity and order to the heritage of earlier ages. It showed Christ surrounded by the sciences, both sacred and secular, thus symbolising the Word, in whom all things subsist :

[1] This was due probably to the misunderstanding of the distinction between λατρεία and προσκύνησις.

"I am the way, the truth, the life." *(John 14 : 6.)* In place of a liturgical or eschatological conception of iconography, Gothic art substitutes a doctrinal and mystical symbolism which brightens the west door of the Gothic cathedrals, and in which different aspects of Christ are united. On the pier, almost level with the faithful, stands a figure of the Good God, with hand uplifted in benediction—"serious and kindly as a teacher, as kindly as a young father" *(Focillon)*. In the heights of the tympanum He presides over the general resurrection and final judgement, no longer the Christ of the Apocalypse, but the Jesus of the Gospels, radiating love, nobility and serenity.

At the end of the sixteenth century the Italian revival introduced a form of art designed to appeal to the emotions rather than to educate or instruct. Influenced by Byzantine monastic art, which was popularised by St. Francis of Assisi, painters began to depict scenes from the life of Jesus of a more homely kind, such as might occur in the ordinary lives of the faithful. Pictures of the baby Jesus snugly lying in His mother's arms became very popular, as also those depicting His passion, hands firmly tied together with a stout cord and a crown of thorns on His head. It was about then that began the devotion of the Stations of the Cross. Franciscan influence was to give rise to a style both picturesque and simple, suitable to the simple workman as well as to the more accomplished artist. The popular style, a heritage of the Middle Ages, was to persist independently of all the great currents of artistic fashion of modern times. It kept to the chief themes of its own choice, scenes from the human life of Jesus, especially the Nativity and Passion.

Today, in reaction against a sterile copying, a popular but long-forgotten Christian art is being recognised as possessing real sincerity and inspiration although somewhat amateurish technically.

A new era began with the Renaissance. After existing for a thousand years the Eastern Empire fell to the invaders, and at about the same time the Renaissance and the Reformation were changing the face of Western Europe. Up till then Christian art had been symbolical or narrative, but sincerity was always prized above formal beauty, the medium being seen as a more striking and durable means of conveying the teaching than mere speech. But the Renaissance introduced especially a more stereotyped style of beauty : the thoughtless copying of the ancient forms dulled all religious sentiment, and although there were still Christian artists there ceased to be any Christian art. With a few notable exceptions the religious art of the Renaissance is no more than ornamental painting. One can admire the works of the period as true masterpieces, but not as examples of religious art. One's religious emotions may be awakened by "The Last Supper" in the Church of Sta. Maria delle Grazie in Milan, but it is difficult to see anything particularly Christian in the thundering Jupiter of "The Last Judgement" in the Sistine Chapel in Rome. It must also be borne in mind that all these religious pictures were intended for the edification of the connoisseurs, not for the instruction of the masses.

The reaction against the over-influence of pagan art came at the Reformation, when the cult of images was put down, and in Protestant countries the representation of our Lord, either in painting or sculpture, was forbidden for centuries. On the other hand, at the catholic Counter-Reformation, the excesses of both Renaissance and popular art were curbed, without condemning the legitimacy of Christian art as such.

Also in modern times one part of Western Christendom produced no pictures of Our Lord, while in the other part two types existed: the first was confused with the History of Art, while the second was responsible for popular works of very differing interest and some religious pictures of very doubtful aesthetic taste.

It was in this period that a new iconographic devotion became popular and world-wide : the devotion to the

Sacred Heart of Jesus. It was the revelations accorded to Margaret Mary Alecoque (1647-1690), a nun in the convent of the Visitation at Paray-le-Monial in central France, that caused the devotion to be raised to a Feast of the whole Roman Catholic Church in the eighteenth century.

It cannot be denied that the artistic expressions of the devotion are often painfully banal, but this is true of much religious art since the Renaissance.

As regards Christian art in the West, certain conclusions emerge:

1. Christ is never pictured with a Semitic face.

2. Both in painting and sculpture Christ's features are always represented as exemplifying the highest ideal of human beauty.

3. Christ is always represented as a white man, usually as a European.

This, however, does not complete the picture. The period immediately after the Renaissance and the end of the Middle Ages was one of startling new voyages and discoveries of new continents, which opened new horizons for the preaching of Christianity. Certain countries outside Europe and the Mediterranean basin, such as parts of Asia and Africa, had been taught Christianity from the time of the Middle Ages, and after the sixteenth century the American continent and Oceania were reached. But of course greatly varying degrees of civilization existed in all these different parts of the world. In Africa, art was primitive and its importance has only become appreciated during this century. The civilizations of the Incas, the Mayas and the Aztecs soon became extinguished before the attacks of the Spanish adventurers. Asia, on the other hand, had long been the cradle of great religions and ancient civilizations. Christian missionaries, therefore, found conditions very different between one country and another. In some they had to adopt the indigenous art to the Gospel message, while in others they had to evolve a wholly new style. "Do not on any pretext try to compel the foreign peoples to change their way of life so long as it is neither dishonest nor clearly contrary to religion. In truth what could be more silly than to try to transplant into China either France, Spain or Italy, or any other part of Europe? That is not your job, which is to bring the faith to these people, a faith which neither repels nor despises the customs and habits of any race, unless, of course, they be immoral, but seeks to treat them with the respect which is their due." (*Collectanea N. 135.*) These wise counsels were seldom heeded, and then they only gave offence to missionaries, who were hidebound by the ideas of the times, and indeed too often weighed down by every kind of worry to have time to give to the development of a native Christian art.

For centuries the mission-field was under European tutelage: a tutelage resented especially in those countries in which ancient civilizations existed, as is shown by the reactions of the Indians, the Chinese and the Japanese. "Christ was an Oriental, but you have turned Him into a European God, that is into a stranger. You push this European religion on to us, westernising everything, philosophy, art, culture and propaganda. And this westernised religion uproots us from our soil, making us strangers in our own land. In short to Indians the innermost beauties and profoundest truths of Christianity are obscured by this European clothing, and are strange and repugnant to us."

In 1925 a University Conference of Chinese Protestants passed a resolution in these terms. "The newly-awakened national self-consciousness of China regards Christianity, as now established in China, as strange to Chinese mentality, and its organisation as being, so many believe, an instrument of imperialist aggression."

Although they may admire our technology, the people of Asia regard Western painting and sculpture as ugly and vulgar. At about the beginning of this century it became realised that the ancient civilisations of Asia could no longer be ignored simply because they were different and pagan. The first Christians in Imperial Rome had been in much the same situation. Just as they had borrowed from Greek and Roman culture, so the Christians of Asia should be able to choose from their own native forms means for the outward expression of an art inspired by the Christian religion.

The times have now changed: colonialism is ended and with the emancipation of a third part of the world, all Christians will in future glorify the one Saviour in the artistic style of their own civilization and culture, whatever that may be.

Native experiments in this direction are too recent to enable a systematic study, such as is possible in the case of the West. All that can be attempted is a description of the first experiments.

CHINA

The first country to be visited by missionaries was China. Nestorian Christians arrived there in the seventh century, but of these very few traces now remain. Others came at the end of the thirteenth century, and of this period we have only very rare objects, namely some Crosses decorated in typically Chinese style. The arrival of Jesuit missionaries at the end of the sixteenth century started a period during which, unfortunately, the development of Chinese Christian art followed a foreign idiom and was without any originality. There were, however, a few attempts at adapting the native style, such as "The Gospel taught in pictures" by Jules Alani in 1635, and the engravings of John Adam Scholl von Bell presented to the Emperor in 1640; also the paintings of G. Castiglione (1688-1766). But, oddly enough, no trace of any portrait of Christ has survived.

Christian art is only a recent development in China, from after the First World War. It is due to Luc Tcheng, professor of art at the catholic University of Peking. He became the centre of a group of Christian painters, who used the delicate spirituality of the traditional Chinese style as a medium for Christian pictures, which are imbued with a poetic freshness reminding one of the masterpieces of the Song dynasty.

What now remains of the painters of Peking, Kaifung and the other Christian churches in China? Has all Christianity and religion been swept away by the red mantle of marxism?

JAPAN

In Japan, neighbour of China and largely influenced by her, the first Christian missionary to arrive was Francis Xavier, in 1549. But the spread of Christianity was soon restricted by persecution and laws prohibiting foreigners from entering Japan. During about the first fifty years European religious art attained a measure of success, probably largely owing to curiosity, but this disappeared later, when nationalist self-reliance and dislike of foreigners developed. Christian art did not really flourish in Japan until after the Second World War. In April, 1952, there was held the first exhibition of Japanese Christian art. Here were exhibited paintings on silk, in full accord with the old national traditions, as well as others showing European influence. This indigenous Christian art is both delicate and tender, and entirely free from affectation. The favourite subjects are episodes from the Gospels and from the lives of the Saints. Japanese artists attach great importance to using the rhythm of movement to convey the spirit of life. A feeling for nature pervades Japanese art, a feeling accepted by Christian artists, whose paintings acquire a spirituality which cannot but stir an echo in any Franciscan heart.

INDO-CHINA

This land of transit was affected from the north by Chinese and from the south by Hindu culture. The pioneer of Christian art was Luc Tran, the architect and builder of the church at Phat Diem. The best-known painter is Celse Le-van-dé. He knew Europe, but remained the faithful interpreter of his people's artistic genius. His art is somewhat influenced by the Chinese, from whom he borrows the sense of line and colour. Here, too, his pictures are full of spiritual significance.

As M. Louis Gillet, of the French Academy, writes, Le-van-dé's paintings "contain that lost quality which is too often forgotten, viz. of tender emotion and spirituality instead of a frigid idealism."

INDIA

The legend which has come down to us that the Apostle Thomas introduced Christianity into India is without historical basis. At the beginning of the sixteenth century the Portuguese arrived in India, bringing Christianity with them. But, as Robert de Nobili (1577-1656) writes, "The Portuguese wanted to turn those they converted not only into Christians but into Portuguese." Just as in China and Japan so in India, Christianity made little headway in combating Hinduism. Here, as elsewhere, it was regarded as an instrument of foreign penetration and an attack on national traditions. "The history of the religion and people of India proves that since Vedic times the soul of Hinduism is full of aspirations which only the Christian revelation can satisfy. But it is essential that the truth be presented to them in a manner suitable to their mental processes, and that neither Christianity nor Christian rites destroy their culture or their customs, which are lawful and right, often admirable." *(Letter from a priest to Celso Constantini.)*

In a vast continent like India the solution of the problem must vary from district to district according to the differing cultures, often confused, which are found. What is needed to restore a Christian art in India is that the art of India should utilize its richness and forms of expression to interpret the Christian aspirations of Indians. A lot has been written on this, and we may hope that the time has passed when Westerners will seek to impose their own ideas on the Christian artists of that vast continent.

Painters were the first to throw off the tutelage of the West. Foremost was Angelo da Fonseca, who was greatly influenced by the "Christa Prema Seva Sangha", an Anglican religious community organised on the Indian model. One of his paintings, "The Nativity", was reproduced in two of Calcutta's important

24

periodicals during the Second World War. "This fact", as Angelo da Fonseca wrote at the time, "makes me think that Hindus would have less difficulty in accepting the mysteries of the Christian faith if these were presented to them in a manner more in keeping with their habits of thought."

Another Indian artist is Alfred Thomas, who was born at Agra, and spent some years studying at the art school at Lucknow. He has painted scenes from the life of Christ and illustrated the Gospel parables. His art, typically Indian, is at once delicate and spiritual. He uses the lotus flower, which means to Indians much what the lily does to Westerners. The paintings of these two, da Fonseca and Thomas, are truly songs without words—Indian songs which can have great charm for us Westerners.

THE INDONESIAN ISLANDS

In these islands—now the Indonesian Republic—indigenous Christian art is quite recent, as in nearly all countries of the far East. Its development is due largely to J. Schmutzer, who writes as follows in *Culture and Christian Art:*

"In 1924 I met the sculptor Iko. His art awoke in me the idea of trying to reawaken the old Indo-Javanese forms, while giving them a Christian interpretation. Iko's sculptures, and those from his studio are well-modelled and not at all realistic. They may be second-rate technically, but they are certainly religiously inspired. In any case indigenous Christian art is very backward in Indonesia."

Starting from Asia, the first pictures of Christ circulated in the West. They acquired that feeling and expression which make them precious in our eyes. Today a new transformation of Christian iconographic art is being worked out in Asia, that cradle of magic civilizations and great religions. The Asiatics will at last express in their art the figure of the Christ who was born and died among them. Paraphrasing the well-known passage in the Acts of the Apostles, they will be able to say : "Chinese, Japanese and Indonesians, and dwellers in the parts between the Ganges and the Indus, Armenians, Nepalese and Thailanders, we hear every man in our own tongue, wherein we were born."

AFRICA

Some Christian missionaries went to countries, such as China, Japan and India, where ancient civilizations existed. Others had their field among peoples sunk in poverty and with little or no civilization. Unlike the Asiatic countries, where the problem was how to adapt existing customs to the Christian life, here the missionaries had to try to educate very primitive peoples as well as preach the Gospel to them. They had, in short, to start right from the bottom in trying to build up a Christian civilization. Missions to Africa are fairly recent : apart from some coastal areas, they do not date before the nineteenth century. These missionaries had but one object : to evangelize, bringing the people to God in Christ. They had, too, all the work of teaching, baptizing, building churches, schools and hospitals; so little time was left to occupy themselves with art—even with Christian art. In any case many of them regarded artistic manifestations—apart from music and singing—as anyhow a mistake, possibly even dangerous, as it was all too easy for their neophytes to regard Christian pictures as the white man's fetishes. Also it was thought that the native arts had lost their traditions and techniques. This was due partly to the decay of the ancient civilizations and cultures, partly to Western influence and the popularity of Western technology and artistic style. The result was that the African natives, who formerly had produced beautiful sculptures, now carved only uncouth and mediocre statuettes.

A certain African missionary thus deplored the condition of his flock's native art: "We Christians have absolutely nothing which can be called an indigenous art. Just a few vulgar fetishes which they like making, and they can neither draw nor make pottery."

But there may well be a revival, for the native Africans have remained artists in the making of household goods, and in decorative art they still have a skill possibly unequalled in the West. Anyhow ideas have greatly changed since the turn of the century. African art is no longer despised as that of an uncultured and inferior race. Systematic research has brought to light much that had long been unknown.

"In Africa, for the most part, one is in the presence of an art deeply integrated in the people's life. It represents a tradition which is often very ancient, but in which later discoveries and influences have been combined, the whole having been slowly evolved in an entirely original way which suits the people's ways of thinking and feeling, and is adapted to a religious and social ideal. These forms of art may be rudimentary, but they are characteristic of the people. It is a humble patrimony, but at least it is their own. And because of this their art often gives a feeling of freshness and vigour." *(Davenson, Ligue Missionnaire, Bulletin des Etudiants de France.)* It is not only in the realm of art that our ideas on Africa are changing, but in the whole mutual relationship of white and black. Through blood and tears, by violence or persuasion, Africa is gradually making her way to freedom and independence. Many Africans hope that their continent may make her own contribution to the emerging civilization, and they know that this will be a long process in which they must preserve their originality while adapting themselves to a rapidly changing world. This ambition, this reawakening of Africa may well, in spite of the present chaos, mark a new start for native Christian communities. In addition, under the pressure of the contemporary world situation the whites realise that they must establish a new relationship with the Africans. A sense of responsibility towards poorer countries is replacing the policies of rule and exploitation existing in former centuries.

In brief, during the era of colonialism foreign influences were too strong to allow the development of an indigenous Christian art. But now, with natives becoming clergymen and filling positions of responsibility, there is emerging an African Christian art—small indeed as yet, but truly authentic. This means that today's situation in Africa is not at all unfavourable to the future of Christianity or of Christian art in this part of the world. The African is a natural sculptor, and the most typical African sculpture is found on the west coast, between Senegal and Angola, and in some parts of the interior, such as the Congo and Tanganyika—also in Madagascar. Particular mention must also be made of the district of Benin, between the Niger and the Congo,

which produces secular statues which are to be found in every art or ethnography gallery in the world. They are of bronze, cast or carved, and of carved wood. There are also similar works of Christian art, but these are not as artistic as the ancient ones from Benin which are well known in Europe. Carving is not as good a medium for illustrating religious themes as painting or drawing. And here we notice a striking difference between Christian art in Asia and in Africa. The Asiatic appears to have a strong predilection for Our Lord's teaching. He is keen to illustrate the parables and episodes in the life of Jesus, the Apostles and the Saints. He has a strong sense of allegory and symbol. The African is quite different. His work represents above all specific objects. He makes a large number of Crucifixes, statuettes of Jesus carrying His Cross, and wooden panels representing the "Stations of the Cross" of Roman Catholic devotion. But always the carvings are native in form and the models used native. Christ is featured as a black man, as also are the women disciples and Pilate and the Roman soldiers. These carvings have certain common features; a restrained nobility, great moderation of expression and a fine feeling for ornamentation. In scenes of the Passion, Pilate's air of a despised ruler is only seen through his hierarchical bearing : Jesus may be bound, but His look is that of one who accepts his condemnation with serene dignity, not that of a wretched criminal. These statuettes of polychrome wood or bronze are small, rather stylised and stiff, but they seem to radiate a sincere, if naive, religious feeling. Although neither as large nor of the artistic merit of the Roman statuary, they are like them in possessing a universal significance.

As regards painting, Christian art in Africa is badly off. The lack of any tradition is obvious, so one must follow with sympathy such beginnings as are being made. The experiments at Cyrene (Southern Rhodesia) and at Makarere (East Africa) are worth noticing. Cyrene is a primary school where African children come from the surrounding districts (Nyasaland, Matabeleland, etc.). In addition to the normal education, two hours a week are set aside for art work. An environment is thus created in which the pupils come naturally to express themselves with paint-brush or chisel. All foreign influences or suggestions are carefully excluded, and every pupil is encouraged to develop his individual talents, influenced only by his native life and surrounding scenery. Certainly only a few pupils succeed in producing anything really worthwhile or continue along this line, but Cyrene has become a small centre of genuine African artistic culture whose reputation has travelled far. The Society for the Propagation of the Gospel has arranged exhibitions of their works in England, and some of their drawings and carvings have reached the United States. Biblical themes are frequently used, and are always treated with local colour. What could be less conventional—and less European—than the Adoration of the Infant Jesus by the shepherds and Magi in the middle of an African landscape?

Apart from its descriptive element, the art of Cyrene shows a freshness which many contemporary artists might envy. Much the same could be written of Makarere College in East Africa, which has pupils belonging to every branch of the Christian Church from Kenya, Tanganyika and Uganda. Christian art in native Africa is rather like the bud of a young branch which has been grafted into the trunk of a wild tree. It will flower and bear fruit only if the trunk remains strong enough. But may not Africa be in danger of losing her soul from contact with a civilization so highly technological as to threaten to impose rigid uniformity on all it embraces? Under the pretext of becoming up-to-date will Africa exchange the promise of a truly native art for the bright trumperies of industrialism?

This book contains some beautiful records of African origin : we must hope that in time artists of that continent will produce some real masterpieces of Christian art.

OCEANIA

The countries of Oceania are widely scattered and cover a vast area. Any detailed investigation would be over-long and produce relatively small results.

In countries like Australia and New Zealand, Christian art was imported by the settlers from Europe. It represents the feelings of the colonisers, not of the natives. In those parts where the natives still live and practise their old customs, there is some hope that a primitive Christian art may grow up. At present there are only rare examples of this, though the Church has a great opportunity here, as in Africa. As in Africa and Asia so in Oceania, such Christian art as exists is inspired by faith, by Gospel texts or some proclamation of God's word. The forms which it takes are as varied as the different local traditions, or the ancient civilizations from which they stem. There are therefore no recognised styles, such as existed in the West in the Middle Ages. Their art is that of craftsmen and artists, encouraged by a missionary Church and not under the influence of theologians or art critics. Each artist has his own language and style in which to set forth the common faith in the redemption of the world by Our Lord, Jesus Christ. So in Asia Christ will be a yellow man, in Africa a black man, also a Bantu among the Bantus, or a Madagascan in Madagascar. There is nothing odd in this, since in other times Christ became Roman, Greek, Russian, French, Spanish and German.

THE AMERICAN CONTINENT

For our present purpose we can count three distinct periods in American history.

The pre-Columbian period is especially characterised by the civilizations of the Mayas and the Aztecs in the centre, and the Incas in the South. The Indians of the North—from Mexico to Alaska—have produced works of art which, though varied and worth attention, are not on the same level with those of the others. This art was, of course, pagan, but it might well, without losing its individuality and style, have become the means of setting forth the great truths of the Faith. The arrival, first of the Spanish adventurers, then of the colonists, completely upset the lives of the inhabitants. Indeed the adventurers found nothing better to do than to exorcise the conquered demons who filled them with such horror and fright. So the ancient civilizations of Central and South America collapsed. In North America the Indians were driven back by the colonists who settled down in different parts in which they soon established themselves with the beliefs, customs and traditions of their country of origin.

Christianity was first introduced into America by the Spaniards and these colonists. To the Indians it was doubly strange. In Latin America religious art not unnaturally copied Spanish or Portuguese baroque styles, to which was added an exuberant and theatrical ornamentation as in the Mexican super-baroque. However, in some distant districts, away from the fountain-head of such imitation, small centres of originality were formed. For instance this happened in New Mexico, where the Spanish Franciscans encouraged native painting and carving. Of that period there remain some statuettes, canvases and painted wooden panels. The composition is borrowed from the European tradition, but the interpretation and feeling are genuinely local.

In the North the colonists had come from England, Scotland, Germany and Norway. They merely imported their own traditions, including the religious belief and habits on account of which they had left their mother country. And it is difficult to say with certainty whether certain objects remaining from that time are American or European. Besides this the different churches and sects, with their very cautious, if not hostile attitude to all pictures or religious decorations, militated against the rise of any really American religious art.

So the period from the discovery of America to the Declaration of Independence in 1776 was one in which the Gospel was preached in many parts till then unknown, but it was not a period which has left us any original legacy, whether from the natives or from the colonists. It was then that all the pre-Columbian heritage and civilizations were neglected or abandoned, if not plundered.

From the end of the nineteenth century a new movement arose in America—especially North America—industrial expansion. Craftsmanship and local skills have been suffocated by mechanization. Most people have abandoned the paint-brush or chisel with the spread of printing and photography; and the same is now happening in Latin America, which has begun to industrialise itself. However, this progress seems to have gone too quickly. In some places there is full expansion, while some large districts have been left to fend for themselves; civilization has passed them by. So there are a number of "islands" where native life has been "civilized" little, if at all. Perhaps some day these regions will give to the Church some Christian art—from the Eskimoes, from the natives of the Magellan Archipelago, or from the Indians round the Amazon forests. At present this is only a hope, for on the occasion of the missionary exhibition held in the Lateran in 1950 it was impossible to collect any objects of merit to witness to the vitality of Christianity among the primitive races of the American continent.

With a few exceptions Christian art has taken much the same course in America as it did in Europe, where in this field, as in many others, it merely copies its country of origin.

*

How then, has mankind striven to create for itself the image of the Christ?

The first Christians, when they wanted to portray the Saviour, were free of any ecclesiastical tradition. This left them independence of action, since no precedent bound them. The Christianity of the early centuries was a youthful cheerful affair, with great powers of assimilation. At one time portraits of Christ made Him like a Roman: He wore the Roman tunic which one finds in His pictures both in the East and the West. Later the Church saw the decay of civilizations in which she had lived, and from each of which she often preserved techniques, forms and styles. And so, gradually, traditions grew up; also fashions. The former became standards of reference, guides: the latter disappeared, frail as are all such as belong to one period only.

So one understands why the new apostles who took the Gospel message to the far ends of the earth were hampered by their traditions and fashions. The lesson of history might be a useful help: equally it might prove a curb. But the universal Church has lost neither the enthusiasm of her early days, nor the power to assimilate and transform, since one sees Christianity developing in Asia and Africa along paths similar to those of the primitive church. Today, as in former days, Christians draw on the treasury of secular art to create an authentic Christian art. These new "early Christians" know that there is no need to alter the existing artistic presentation of Christianity to suit Japanese or Buddhist mentality. Their faith and courage will lead them to create a Japanese, Indian or African art which, in the eyes of their compatriots, Christian or non-Christian, will bear witness to Christ's universal message of love.

And above all it must be remembered that the creation of Christian art is not the Church's chief task, which is to obey her Lord's command : "Go ye therefore, and teach all nations, baptizing them in the name of the Father, and of the Son, and of the Holy Ghost." *(Matthew 28 : 19.)* Also many Christian churches have forbidden some figures of Christ, either for theological reasons, or on grounds of pastoral prudence, knowing how prone men are to attach over-importance to the physical pictures of God to the detriment of faith in Him alone.

Twenty centuries of Christianity have, however, produced a large number of pictorial representations of Christ. He has been shown as a Greek, a Roman, a Syrian and a Byzantine. He has been featured as a Slav and as a Westerner; of both yellow and black race. Also, He is shown as serious and majestic; serene or pitifully human; bright in glory or tender as a baby in His mother's arms. In all these different pictures He is always the Christ. For, shining through the artist's work Christians recognize—as if instinctively—the divine figure, the apotheosis of the human soul's noblest desires.

There is, surely, no occasion to regret that the first centuries of the Christian era did not leave us any true or authentic portrait of the Christ. Is it not perhaps more suitable to our human condition that we have not been left one? A definitely authentic portrait would have fixed for all time what were the features of the Saviour. It may be better that man, throughout the ages, should meditate on His teaching, and seek to find, in the depths of his own soul, a vision of the Christ he has learned by faith. Gerard Hauptman wrote:

"He who would dare paint the portrait of the Man wearing the Crown of Thorns, he must give thereto his whole life . . . not just a troubled or arrant existence : he must give hours, days, years of solitude and contemplation. He must be alone with his sorrows, with his God. He must be free from any evil or contamination. Having so struggled and suffered, the Holy Spirit may come to him. Then he will see a vision, he will rest in eternity . . . and then serene and beautiful, unwilled by him, he will see the Saviour. He is there."

THE CHILDHOOD OF JESUS

The events of Christ's life most commonly featured pictorially are His Infancy and His Passion.

His birth and everything connected with it—the flight into Egypt and Jesus' secluded life with His parents in Nazareth—are almost inexhaustible springs of inspiration. It is, therefore, practically impossible to draw up a complete list of the works produced on this theme in twenty centuries of Christianity.

As this book does not pretend to be an exhaustive study, we will not give an inventory of Christian iconography relating to the Infancy. We will simply point out the most important subjects, try to explain how they originated, and, in some cases, give a sketch of their probable evolution.

In the primitive Church, a saint's anniversary was observed, not on the date of his birth, but of his death or, more correctly, of his heavenly birth. The same practice is observed in the Roman Catholic martyrology. This explains why, for a long time, the glorious feast of Easter was considered the greatest of the Christian year. In A.D. 353 Pope Liberius fixed December 25 for the celebration of Our Lord's Nativity; this is now the accepted traditional date and for centuries has been the established custom.

As the feast of Christmas was relatively late in gaining a place in the liturgy, so also was the appearance of pictures of Christ's Infancy. The feast of Christmas was first introduced by the Eastern Church. The Emperor Constantine, who died in A.D. 337, built, in addition to the churches of Golgotha (Martyrium) and the Holy

Sepulchre (more correctly Anastasis or Resurrection) in Jerusalem, another church (the Church of the Holy Nativity) at Bethlehem, on the very spot where the Blessed Virgin had given birth to Jesus. Constantine's mother, Helena, presented a silver crib to the church, which became a famous object for pilgrimages.

After the middle of the fourth century the Roman Church of Santa Maria Maggiore became a centre of Christmas celebrations, as the feast's importance increased in the liturgical calendar. As the centuries elapsed, Christmas became a very popular feast: songs and hymns, cribs, Mystery Plays, all showed a popularity that still persists. But when were cribs first made? In the Lateran Museum there is a mid-fourth-century sarcophagus in which one sees Jesus, wrapped in swaddling clothes, lying in a cot that is placed on the roof of a stable, and standing round are an ox and a donkey.

It is interesting to compare these very old representations of the Nativity with the Gospel texts. St. Luke's account is very brief. He writes *(2 : 7)*, "And she brought forth her firstborn son, and wrapped him in swaddling clothes, and laid him in a manger; because there was no room for them in the inn." St. Matthew just alludes to the birth, which neither St. Mark nor St. John even mention.

The Lateran sarcophagus gives more detail, as an ox and a donkey figure in it. Christian art sought to supplement the extremely brief Gospel accounts with allegory and details by which the faithful could be taught and edified.

But closer examination shows that, from the first, two different conceptions affected the treatment of the Nativity theme. In the pictures emanating from Syria, and later Byzantium, the Virgin is lying down, showing the close tie between her and her Child. This is not so apparent in Greek Nativities, where she is sitting down.

The Christian East (Syria, Byzantium) treat the Nativity as a perfectly normal delivery. The Virgin is doleful and lies stretched out; the Child has been given to one or more midwives for His first bath. This theme was common until the eve of the Reformation. (It is worth noticing that Eastern art of the pre-Reformation period would not depict the sufferings of Jesus on the Cross. They clearly made a distinction between the "natural" pains of a woman in childbirth and the "extraordinary" sufferings of a God on the Cross.)

In the West, on the other hand, from the end of the Middle Ages, the Nativity as an Adoration gradually replaced the theme of the Nativity as a normal delivery. Here the Virgin is on her knees, with hands joined, and the Child is lying before her, either on a bundle of straw or the folds of her cloak.

This brief account of the two different Nativity themes has necessarily meant ignoring those numberless details that give such charm and atmosphere to the many Nativity pictures.

THE NORMAL-DELIVERY NATIVITY

The setting is what we should expect: a cave, both stable and living place. The Newly Born, carefully swathed, is lying by His mother's side. Sometimes she is shown giving Him the breast. Joseph is just a figure, either sitting in a corner, or helping with a few odd jobs. Many of these details are taken from the Mystery Plays, which flourished during the Middle Ages.

Soon new figures appear, in addition to the traditional ones. First were the midwives. Many legends grew up about them. Byzantine art gives them names—Zelomi and Maia. Zelomi, having actually assisted at the birth, testifies that the mother remained a virgin after the delivery. Maia, however, is incredulous. Like Thomas in St. John's Gospel, she wants to see and to touch. But her hand starts to wither and she is cured only after she touches Jesus' swaddling clothes.

It seems strange to us that the midwives should be present, as they are not mentioned in Scripture, but only in the Apocryphal Gospels. There is, however, a fairly clear reason for their persistent presence, namely, to have two expert witnesses to prove Christ's supernatural birth. It was in vain that St. Jerome decried both their presence and the need for it: popular credulity continued their existence in all iconographic art until the sixteenth century.

The midwives' preparation for Jesus' first bath seems to weaken somewhat their evidence of His supernatural birth. If Jesus was, in fact, born of a virgin, He was uncontaminated and needed no washing.

So the bath scene, as well as the presence of the midwives, was abandoned for two reasons. First, on doctrinal grounds: according to the belief that was gradually gaining ground at the close of the Middle Ages, the Virgin's delivery was painless, and the Adoration Nativity made the presence of the midwives of the Normal-Delivery Nativity unneccessary. They disappeared. The second reason was an aesthetic one: it seemed out of place to show, in the same picture, Jesus all wrapped in swaddling clothes lying by His mother's side, and also being handled, naked, by midwives. The subject of a religious picture must be single, easily identifiable and, of course, in conformity with the Church's teaching.

THE ADORATION NATIVITY

A new theme, the Adoration Nativity, appears in Christian iconographic art from about the fourteenth century; this Nativity was thought to be more in conformity with the Church's beliefs. This theme presents the Child naked and radiant. Mary and Joseph are on their knees in adoration of the God-Child. Historians of religious art give many reasons for this very radical change, but none are more than hypotheses. There was the influence of certain saints, such as the mystic St. Bridget of Sweden (c. 1303-1373) and, possibly, St. Bernard (1090-1153). Most important was the increase in popular devotion to the Virgin. The faithful saw in her a specially privileged witness to her Son's divinity and a perfect example of Christian faith. This new form of picturing the Nativity spread throughout Christendom and still persists.

In Asiatic and African countries, one must expect some innovations. Already the Japanese, Kosaki Kimoko, has departed from traditional orthodoxy. He makes the Virgin herself wash her new-born Son, thus going back to the theme of the Child's bath, which had disappeared in the sixteenth century.

A much simpler crib is the anonymous African one, in which only three people appear: Jesus, Mary, and Joseph. The technique is certainly primitive, but it has deep religious feeling and is similar to the old Byzantine style. The Nativity theme may again be in process of transformation, owing to the influence of the newer countries, but it will not necessarily lose the charm that so endears the festival of Christmas to everyone.

Through the centuries, the development of the Nativity theme has produced some highly significant secondary characters. The Adoration Nativity is closely associated with the worship of the angels, the shepherds, and the Magi, not to mention that of the ox and the donkey.

Angels took their place in Nativity pictures following the angel of the Lord who brought the news to the shepherds *(Luke 2 : 8 et seq.)*. Towards the end of the Middle Ages and the Baroque period the presence of angels increased enormously. Some were pictured as astonished worshippers, others as singers and musicians. Their presence has a certain basis, as the Gospel mentions them, whereas the ox and the donkey are referred to only in an Apocryphal Gospel of the sixth century, pseudo-Matthew: "The Virgin laid her son in a cradle, and the ox and the ass enclosed him. Thus was fulfilled the prophecy of Isaiah 'the ox and the ass knew their master.'" All kinds of explanations were used to justify the presence of these animals. In countries where there were no donkeys, e.g. Russia, horses replaced them. It is pertinent to ask what will happen in countries with neither oxen nor donkeys. Will the use of animals disappear, or will the traditional ones be replaced by buffaloes and antelopes, as is already occurring in some popular African pictures?

The events described in the Gospel—the angels' message to the shepherds found in both Byzantine and Western art during the Middle Ages, and the worship of the Magi—are the earliest to be pictured. The shepherds' worship, sometimes alone, sometimes together with that of the Magi, is not used until about the fifteenth century. Theologians and artists had to fill out the details in the Lucan text, both to satisfy the curiosity of the faithful and to prevent a host of absurd details. A usual scene depicts three shepherds prostrate before the Child, who lies naked in His crib: the shepherds symbolise the Jews. One offers the best lamb of the flock, symbolising the Saviour's own sacrifice; the second his crook, signifying that the Child will become the shepherd of souls; the third offers his pipe, signifying that, like a new Orpheus, our Lord will draw disciples to Himself. Later, the shepherds will be joined by two shepherd-girls who bring milk, poultry, and eggs—produce of the soil and humble offerings of the common people.

The Adoration of the Shepherds symbolised the worship of all ordinary folk round the crib. The scene recalled was one that they had often experienced in their own lives, and it was a source of help and comfort to know that Providence associated them with the most important event of all time, the Saviour's birth.

No wonder that this subject is found everywhere, on the porches of churches, in stained-glass windows, in prayer-books, and later, in all the profusion of the south, in the cradles of Naples and Provence.

The account of the Magi is not given in St. Luke's Gospel, but in that of St. Matthew *(2 : 1-12)*. A large number of Apocryphal Gospels have supplemented St. Matthew's account, e.g., the Protevangelium of James *(Chap. 21)*, the Gospel of pseudo-Matthew *(Chap. 16)*, and the Arabian Infancy Gospel *(Chap. 7)*. St. Matthew tells us neither the number nor the names of the Magi: he writes simply "there came wise men from the East," and "they presented unto him gifts; gold, and frankincense, and myrrh."

In traditional iconography the Magi, now kings, were three in number, and their names were Caspar, Melchior, and Balthasar. They had come from the three then-known continents, Asia, Africa, and Europe. The explanation and the growth of this theme are extremely interesting. In the first place, it is a very old story, found in the Capella Graeca of the Catacomb of Priscilla in Rome (second century), and on the canopy of the cubicle of the catacomb of St. Peter (third century).

Christian art borrowed the motif of the triumphal arch, first the Roman and later the Byzantine. At this time,

the Adoration of the Magi was not intended to picture an actual scene from Christ's life, but was regarded as symbolising His divinity. The earthly kings had come to pay homage to the King of Kings. Then gradually the symbol was forgotten, and this event, embellished with a crowd of picturesque details, turned into a spectacle.

But what decided the number of the Magi, or turned them into kings, or made them representatives of the continents of Asia, Africa, and Europe? At first, their number varied considerably, sometimes two, sometimes four. In the Syrian Church there were even twelve, after the twelve tribes of Israel.

The number three was finally accepted because St. Matthew mentions three gifts presented to Jesus—gold, frankincense, and myrrh. Gold signifies the homage due to Christ as King, incense pays honour to His divinity and myrrh to His mortality. The number three also gave rise to many symbolical speculations: the three Magi could represent the three ages of man; the three parts of the then-known world; or the descendants of Noah's three sons, Shem, Ham, and Japheth. One of these symbolical explanations had to be abandoned when America was discovered, but by then the iconographic fashion was too well-established to be affected.

Rather late, in A.D. 845, the names of the Magi appear in the Pontifical of Ravenna, and popular folklore has kept the names. St. Matthew called them "wise men," and later they became kings. In truth, they were probably just ordinary astrologers, but as the word "magi" (or wise men) and "magician" have the same root, and, as the latter is often used pejoratively, they were made kings so as to restore their dignity. Tertullian was responsible for the change.

In the fifteenth century, the scene of the Adoration of the Magi had become a *tableau vivant*, an excuse for flattering patrons and important people. One has seen many Magi with the features of a Valois, a Duke of Burgundy, or a Medici. However, we can ignore these matters, which have nothing to do with Christian art.

In the oldest examples, the Virgin has her Child on her knees, thereby serving as His living throne. This detail of composition is nearly always followed. In early times, the Virgin and Child, seen in profile, greet the Magi as these pass before them. Later, the Virgin and Child are placed, full-faced, in the centre of the picture, a position of greater dignity. In the oldest pictures, the Child is swathed; later, He is naked but made to look older than in pictures of the Adoration of the Shepherds; finally, He wears a tunic.

Sometimes He is blessing the Magi, sometimes stroking their horses or their beards, and sometimes He is handling their gifts. According to tradition, the Magi represent the Gentiles, and also all the great ones of this world.

In some rather late compositions, the Adoration of the Shepherds and the Adoration of the Magi are shown together, and here the shepherds occupy a less prominent place in the canvas. Several contemporary African artists have chosen just this composition. In a typically African design, from which the cave of Bethlehem is absent, Jesus, sitting in His mother's lap, receives the homage of all Africa, represented by the shepherds, the Magi, and many types of animals—donkeys, buffaloes, lambs, and even antelopes. African painters have rediscovered the old symbolism of the scene: Jesus is acknowledged as King of Kings.

By the Mosaic law, a male child had to be circumcised and given a name on the eighth day after his birth; on the fourteenth day, the mother had to be purified and the child presented to God. St. Luke's Gospel tells us that Jesus and Mary submitted humbly to this provision of the law.

For a long time, these two events inspired a definite type of iconography. In fact, the Circumcision (or Feast of the Holy Name of Jesus) is no longer depicted, but it must be admitted that from the fifth century (in a miniature in the Menologe of Basil) until the nineteenth century, the art inspired by this passage from Holy Scripture, even when painted by great artists, was not always in the best of taste.

As the rite of circumcision was usually performed in the temple by a specially trained priest, the two events—the feasts of the Circumcision and the Presentation—both placed in the same setting, became confused. To avoid the confusion, or possible conflation of the two, one was gradually given up. The Presentation, obviously more suitable for artistic representation, gradually ousted the Circumcision.

In any event, St. Luke gave a detailed account of the Presentation of Jesus in the Temple, or the Purification of the Blessed Virgin Mary, an account which gave rise to a devotion, and therefore to an iconography of its own. Let us recall the scene. Mary—Joseph remains throughout in the background—goes to the Temple to present Jesus to the Lord, "As it is written in the law of the Lord. Every male that openeth the womb shall be called holy to the Lord," and also to offer the sacrifice, "A pair of turtledoves, or two young pigeons." Here we have two distinct scenes, the presentation of Jesus Himself, and Mary's offering of the sacrifice. But the Gospel also records how the aged Simeon, taking Jesus in his arms, blessed God and said:

> "Lord now lettest thou thy servant depart in peace, according to thy word:
> For mine eyes have seen thy salvation
> Which thou hast prepared before the face of all people;
> A light to lighten the Gentiles, and the glory of thy people Israel."

And immediately after he said to Mary:

> "Behold, this *child* is set for the fall and rising again of many in Israel; and for a sign which shall be spoken against; (Yea, a sword shall pierce through thy own soul also), that the thoughts of many hearts may be revealed."

It was this prophecy—"Yea, a sword shall pierce through thy own soul"—that started the devotion of the Seven Sorrows of the Blessed Virgin Mary. A corresponding iconographic fashion also sprang up, which achieved great popularity in Europe, but is not found in mission countries.

Pictures of the Presentation became current from the fifth century, but seemed gradually to give place to Our Lord's Baptism, which was more akin to the Christian ritual than the survival of a Jewish rite, and was familiar in everyday Christian life.

According to St. Matthew, 2: 13-15, the Flight into Egypt took place immediately after the departure of the Magi. As early as the eighth century, this event is pictured in scenes from Christ's life.

St. Matthew's very matter-of-fact account of the flight has been embroidered in countless ways by the Apocryphal Gospels and the Golden Legend. Homely and picturesque details inspired the story-tellers of the Middle Ages, and certainly a large proportion of these tales belong to a past so typically European as to have no interest for the non-European Christian artist. Even in Europe this tradition has now been almost completely forgotten; though poetical and tender, it was often puerile.

Three people figure in the scene of the Flight into Egypt: the Child Jesus, Mary, and Joseph.

The commonest scene depicts Joseph leading a donkey, on which the mother and Child ride. Across his shoulder Joseph carries a stick with a small bundle. In the Middle Ages, the bundle was depicted as a cask of water, or even of wine, from which Joseph could refresh himself from time to time. In other pictures one sees Joseph casting looks of loving solicitude on mother and Child. The donkey is not always in the picture; the fugitives sometimes go on foot, with Jesus either on Joseph's shoulders, or trotting along between Mary and Joseph. A Chinese artist of the school of Peking, Lu-Hung-Nien, has incorporated a picturesque detail showing the fugitives crossing a river in a barge, though this may be taken either from an old European Christian tradition or from a pagan Chinese one. Another Chinese artist, Li-Ning-Yuen, shows Joseph leading the donkey by a rein as the three enter a river that they are about to ford. In this instance, Joseph is turning round to speak words of encouragement to his companions.

The African, Justin Accrumbessi, has rediscovered the great qualities of the sculptors of Benin in his bronze group of "The Flight into Egypt." Its simplicity and dignity are out of all proportion to its small size.

Pictures of the Blessed Virgin, which are not always welcome in some Christian churches, are numerous, but interest us only where Jesus is also included.

Byzantine art again furnishes the two principal styles, the majestic Virgin and the tender, motherly Virgin.

The first style, probably dating back to the fourth century, may have been obtained by taking the mother and Child out of the Adoration of the Magi, where they are central. These sculptures, and this style was first represented in sculpture, are numerous, especially from the beginning of the Roman period, about the eleventh century. The Virgin is seated, full-face. Her expression is serious and her bearing almost hieratic. The Child Jesus sits on her knees, but she seems quite detached from her Son: she is just Jesus' living throne. Jesus, too, looks majestic, and one wonders whether one is looking at the Child Jesus or Christ the King. He seldom has the build of a child, and never a childlike look. His whole being, including His hand raised in benediction, is rather that of One who has said "My kingdom is not of this world." If it be correct that these derive from the Adoration of the Magi, there is nothing surprising in their style.

For the severity of expression, Gothic art substituted expressions of motherly tenderness and child-love. These take so many shades of feeling that it is not really possible to enumerate all the different types. However, it can be said that in the Middle Ages it was rare to see a smile on Mary's face. It is Jesus who smiles up to her as He reaches forward to her embraces. The Virgin wears a worried expression: possibly she knows that she is to lose her Child; or does she realise the immense differences separating her, a creature, from Jesus, the Son of God? Even before the Renaissance this manner of portraying the Virgin reached such a pitch that the painting of Madonnas became an excuse for portraits and conversation-pieces, whose only connection with religion lay in the outward details, i.e., the right number of characters. For example, Raphael's Madonnas, great masterpieces though they be, have little connection with Christian art, properly understood.

This very popular subject of the Madonna occasioned a number of excellent works many of which are unknown, and hidden in some museum or country church. But a lot of the sculpture and painting was—as it still is—in very questionable, if not frankly bad, taste.

Especially in the Catholic missionary countries, the religious Christian art is prolific in Madonnas. Africa produces some statuettes of polychrome wood, which are restrained and entirely worthy of being in a church, and there are also some nice watercolours in Asia. But, with a few exceptions, they lack that subtlety necessary to make a mere picture of motherhood into a true Christian Madonna.

The devotion to the Holy Family—Jesus, Mary, and Joseph—was unknown in the Middle Ages, and first appeared in the art of the time of the Counter-Reformation, which favoured the development of the cult of the Holy Family. The celebration of this feast, on the first Sunday after the Epiphany, was instituted in the Roman Catholic Church in 1921.

The Holy Family was enlarged to include Anne, the mother of Mary, and John the Baptist, Jesus' cousin. These family portraits became domestic scenes of life at Nazareth. Mary would be spinning, Joseph at his carpenter's bench, and Jesus either playing or doing little odd jobs. The artist could draw his inspiration from one or another of the numberless popular legends that filled the gap left by the meagre Gospel accounts of this period of Jesus' life.

This theme produced no great works, but the large number of engravings and small paintings show that it caught the popular imagination.

Sometimes, too, Jesus is shown accompanied by Joseph, by St. Antony of Padua, or by St. Christopher. Sometimes He is playing with a cross, as if His thoughts were turned towards the coming dark hours of His Passion. The infant Jesus, in His helplessness and innocence, attracts and has attracted men everywhere. That the Child is the Son of God, comes down from Heaven and becomes poor and a fugitive for man, adds to this natural attraction. So artists of every country and tradition have sought to represent the scenes of His Childhood. Details will vary according to time and place, but these are of no moment, as long as they are all based on the simple Gospel text: "And she brought forth her firstborn son, and wrapped him in swaddling clothes, and laid him in a manger; because there was no room for them in the inn."

And Christians, the world over, proclaim that Son to be the Saviour of the World.

THE ADORATION OF THE ASS AND THE OX — SWITZERLAND

This adoration by the ox and the ass, characteristically franciscan in feeling, is painted on the roof of the Church at Zillis, in Switzerland. It is based on a very old and still popular legend, which is, however, without Scriptural basis. A symbolical meaning used to be attached to the animals: the ox, with his neck in a yoke, symbolised the Jew, still bound to the Law; the ass, a beast of burden, symbolised the pagan still under the burden of idolatry. Possibly the artist, in the spirit of Poverello, wanted to associate "brother ox" and "brother ass' in the joy of the first Christmas night.

43

This "Nativity" reminds one of a simple country birth under a tropical African sky. Of a realistic piety, it combines two different conceptions of the Nativity. The first, commonly followed in the Eastern Church, depicted the Nativity as a normal human birth, with the usual accompanying pains; the second, followed in the West from the fifteenth century, stressed the adoration of the new-born Child.

In the second picture, Mary presents her Son to God; Joseph brings the pair of turtledoves, the offering of the poor. The aged Simeon, taking the Child in his arms, says the Nunc Dimittis, "Lord, now lettest thou thy servant depart in peace," and the kneeling Mary hears the dreadful prophecy, "Yea, a sword shall pierce through thy own soul also".

The people of Barcelona have seen this scene depicted on a keystone of a vault of their cathedral for the last six hundred years or more.

AN AFRICAN CRIB — IVORY COAST

44

THE PRESENTATION — BARCELONA

Some Nativity pictures depart from historical realism in order the better to express the spirit of Christmas. Both in the drawing by a Japanese lady artist and in the anonymous painting one gets the feeling of the enormous love which surrounds both humans and inanimate objects on this happy Christmas night. The contrast between the simplicity of the Japanese Nativity and the magnificence of the European Adoration of the Magi underlines the differences between their civilizations, but such differences do not hinder all Christian souls from sharing in the mystery of the birth of a Saviour who came into the world to save all men, rich and poor, high and low, of whatever race and colour.

THE NATIVITY, BY KOSEKI KIMICO — JAPAN   THE ADORATION OF THE MAGI — FRANCE

Worshipping angels appear only late in Western tradition. The first to be pictured was the messenger who took the news of our Lord's birth to the shepherds. Later one sees an angel carrying the star that led the Magi to the stable. Gradually their number multiplies, especially in the fifteenth century. Crowds of child-angels kneel before the Babe; sometimes, in joyful exuberance, they perform an aerial dance or give a choral and orchestral concert, or, perching like a team of sparrows on the roof of the stall, they sing the "Gloria in excelsis".

THE CHILD AND THE ANGELS — GERMANY   THE ADORATION OF THE MAGI — RHODESIA

However much the details may vary, there are three characters who are always shown in pictures of the Flight into Egypt, the Child Jesus, the Virgin Mary and Joseph. This Chinese artist has kept to the tradition, but in his treatment follows the old Chinese masters, while the African that of the native genius of his own country. Both are deeply religious in inspiration.

THE FLIGHT INTO EGYPT,
BY LI-MING-YUEN — CHINA

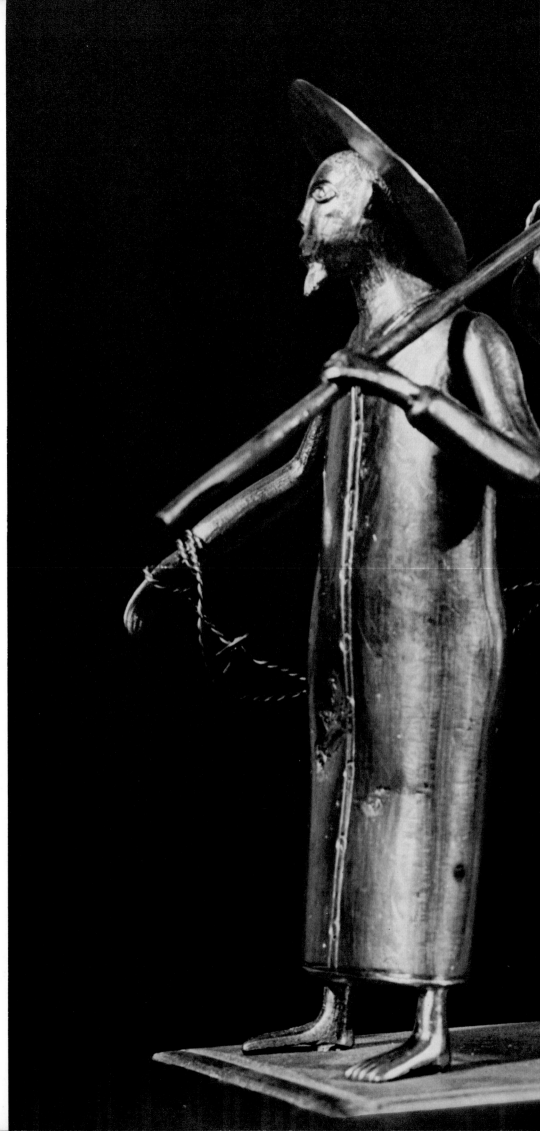

THE FLIGHT INTO EGYPT,
BY JUSTIN ACCROMBESSI — WEST AFRICA

VIRGIN AND CHILD, BY DAVID CHITUKU – RHODESIA

VIRGIN AND CHILD, BY VANTHO – VIET-NAM

VIRGIN AND CHILD, BY WOELLFEL – WEST AFRICA

An ancient fourth-century bas relief of the Adoration of the Magi, shows Jesus accompanied by Mary, His Mother. And later Byzantine art supplied the West with many such designs. The portrayals of Jesus with Mary follow two different styles: those in which the Blessed Virgin is represented as a majestic figure, and those in which she is shown as a motherly and tender woman. The first prevailed in Europe from the eleventh century, the second in the Gothic and Baroque periods.

The Majestic Virgins are generally carved, and shown full face, sitting on a throne with Jesus on their knees. Their expressions are severe and their carriage very stately.

But with the Motherly Virgins one sees portrayed the love which existed between Jesus and His mother. Artists all over the world have treated this theme with great feeling, for it has a world-wide appeal. Also these outnumber the Majestic Virgins. One of the oldest to originate outside Europe is this painted wooden carving of the Virgin, an instance of the popular art developed among the peoples of New Mexico by Spanish Franciscan missionaries.

The author of this motherly Virgin, a Korean, has called it "Confidence". Jesus' calm gaze and Mary's serene yet humble bearing create a feeling of tranquil simplicity. This treatment of the Virgin and Child is full of religious value, in spite of their somewhat exotic clothing.

THE VIRGIN AND CHILD – SWITZERLAND

THE HOLY FAMILY, BY ONDO FLORIN – NIGERIA

This majestic Virgin was carved in lime wood about the end of the twelfth century: serenely royal, almost hieratic, she acts as a living throne for the Christ. Formerly an object of veneration, it is now a museum-piece, a pious relic of a different past.

Eight centuries separate this Holy Family from the Romanesque sculpture which is opposite. Although the African artist was almost completely ignorant of medieval European art, there is a striking likeness between the two Virgins: the same simplicity of technique accompanied by deep religious feeling. They are both primitive: the one reminds us of the past, the other marks perhaps the beginning of a new era of Christian art. Certainly the carving of Joseph shows a general tendency towards an African expressionism.

In his *Spiritual Conferences* St. Francis of Sales wrote that Mary, Jesus and Joseph formed an earthly trinity in some way analogous to the Holy Trinity. At the time, i. e. that of the Counter Reformation, this idea became popular in European iconography, and, developing into the cult of the Holy Family, has remained so. It was spread by the Spanish missionaries in America, as can be seen from this "retable" or panel, which was painted in the country around New Mexico. The elegant folds of the draperies and the drawing of the arms show the inborn artistic sense of the painter, but yet he is curiously simple. Jesus, being the most important person present, is drawn as tall as His parents, but because His still a child, the artist makes His hands very small. Age has not diminished the charm of this primitive work.

THE PUBLIC MINISTRY

Only one event that occurred between the return of Jesus and His family from Egypt to Nazareth and the beginning of His public ministry has been recorded in the Gospels, and that is His meeting with the Doctors in the midst of the Temple at Jerusalem, when He was twelve years old. Jesus had gone up to Jerusalem with His parents for the Feast of the Passover, but instead of going back to Nazareth with them, He had stayed behind. St. Luke *(2 : 41 et seq.)* records that after a day's journey from Jerusalem, Joseph and Mary realised that Jesus was not with them, and turned back to look for Him. They found Him "in the temple, sitting in the midst of the doctors, both hearing them and asking them questions. And all that heard him were astonished at his understanding and answers."

This is the first account of Jesus as Teacher. It is depicted rarely in primitive Christian art, but very often in that of the sixteenth and seventeenth centuries. Probably the theological disputes of that period explain the popularity of this episode, which shows Jesus as both the teacher and the pupil—the disciple correcting His masters. Today the scene has lost its popularity, except in present-day India. That country, where masters and teachers of religion and wisdom are so numerous, is possibly more responsive to so unusual a situation. Here is not a man who has learnt wisdom after many years of meditation and mystic contemplation, but a God-Child expounding the supreme wisdom.

Jesus, the youth, is usually portrayed sitting down, though sometimes He is standing, more like someone preaching to others than "sitting in the midst of the doctors, both hearing them and asking them questions," as in the Gospel. Always in the centre of the picture, He is not "asking questions" of the doctors, but teaching them. They listen attentively: some perplexed, some questioning, and some just plainly astonished at the Child's wisdom. Joseph and Mary usually appear in the background, and look equally astonished, although possibly not for quite the same reasons. This episode in Christ's life is mentioned only by St. Luke, but the Baptism of Jesus in the Jordan is recorded in all four Gospels.

Originally, the Baptism of Jesus was commemorated on January 6, the Epiphany. The Apostolic Constitutions, dating from the last half of the fourth century, say in regard to this feast, "This day must be accepted, for it is that on which Christ's divinity was revealed, when the Father bore witness to Him, and the Holy Spirit appeared over His head in the form of a dove."

And today, the Coptic Church retains this old meaning of the Feast of the Epiphany, while the West, by associating it with the Adoration of the Magi, has given it a derivative meaning: the manifestation of Christ to the Gentiles. The pictorial representations of the Gospel story of the Baptism have varied greatly, since the episode is both an event in the life of Jesus and the basis of Christian baptism. As the Gospels give few details, the iconography has developed parallel with that of the liturgy of the sacrament.

In the first centuries, in order to follow Christ's example, the Church baptised people by total immersion in a river or swimming-pool. This gave rise to an anomaly. How is it that Jesus, then thirty years old, is pictured as a child? The explanations given show how liturgical considerations influenced artistic ones. Two were suggested: first in the liturgy the candidate is called "puer," which means child, or secondly by this time the Church had begun to baptise infants.

The first picture of the Baptism showing Jesus as a grown-up is in the Syriac Gospel of Rabula, which is now in the Laurentian Library in Florence. From then on, i.e., the end of the sixth century, pictures of the Baptism show Jesus as a grown man.

Another instance of the influence of the liturgy on art is that now Jesus is shown, not as being immersed in the Jordan, but as being baptised in a basin. As a matter of convenience, the Church had to abandon the practice of immersion in running water in place of still water poured beforehand into a basin.

In the pictures showing baptism by immersion, Jesus is naked and the water rises to His waist or to His armpits. For reasons of modesty the water is not transparent, but ripples on its surface show it to be flowing.

An enamel retable of Nicholas of Verdun (1181), to be seen at Klosternenburg, near Vienna, marks an iconographic and liturgical change. For the first time, one sees Jesus standing in the waters of the Jordan and at the same time being sprinkled by John the Baptist. This brings together two methods of baptism, the traditional one of immersion, and the newer one of aspersion. Ever since the fourteenth century the Western Church has used the aspersion method of baptism in her liturgy, and this was followed in the iconography.

In the pictures of baptism by aspersion, Jesus is shown standing in the water, thus following the Gospel records. Instead of the water, a loin-cloth conceals His nakedness. John the Baptist stands either in the water or in a barge on the water, and pours water over Jesus' head, sometimes using his cupped hand, sometimes a shell or jug.

At the time of the Renaissance, the Baptism had become just a pretext for pictures that were not in the least religious: the sacrament was turned into a bathing-party scene, and Raphael even introduces this sort of scene in his Vatican frescoes.

After the Council of Trent, the Church tried to stop these pictures, which were just a profanation of religious subjects. As a sign of His humility, Jesus began to be portrayed not in the water, but in a barge, clothed and kneeling before John the Baptist. However by this time, artists, like philosophers and men of science, had won a freedom from clerical interference that they did not enjoy in the Middle Ages, and so the influence of the Council of Trent was not widespread.

To sum up, the development of the Baptism theme may thus be stated briefly:

1. Christ is immersed naked in the River Jordan, and John the Baptist places his hand on His head.
2. Christ, clad in a loin-cloth, stands upright on the river-bed, with the water covering His ankles. John the Baptist pours the water on to His head.
3. Christ, wearing a tunic, humbly kneels before John the Baptist, who baptises Him by aspersion.

The Baptism was the starting-point of Jesus' public ministry, being a guarantee of its authenticity. So John the Baptist, when he heard the voice from heaven, "This is my beloved Son, in whom I am well pleased," (*Matthew 3: 17;* and see *Mark 1: 11, Luke 3: 22*) bore his own witness, "And I saw, and bare record that this is the Son of God" (*John 1: 34*). But before starting to preach the Word of God, Jesus submitted to the Temptations. Three particular ones are described in Matthew and Luke: first, to use His power as the Son of God to turn stones into bread in order to satisfy His hunger after a fast of forty days; secondly, to cast Himself down from a pinnacle of the Temple, i.e., to put God to an arbitrary test and to stage a spectacular miracle; and thirdly, to obtain from the devil power over all the kingdoms of the world by falling down and worshipping him, i.e., to desert His true mission for the sake of power unworthily obtained. The Temptations became an iconographic theme only in the Carolingian period, and they then caused some difficulty, for how was the artist to depict both Jesus and the devil together? Oddly enough it was with the devil that there was the most difficulty. Some artists represented him in the shape of a monstrous beast, others under human disguise. Christ, whose iconographic type had by this time become settled, either stands or sits, but His attitude never leaves any doubt that the tempter has failed.

As a subject for art, the Temptations went out of fashion in the West, but it is interesting to note that there are some examples in Asia and Africa today. A possible explanation lies in the analogy between Christ's Temptations and that of Buddha, and also in the belief in evil spirits, a belief shared by Hindus and Africans alike.

And was not belief in the devil stronger in the Middle Ages than now?

After His Baptism and Temptation, Jesus chose His apostles and started on His journeys through Judea, Samaria, and Galilee, preaching as He went. He left no writings, His teaching being completely oral. But through the Gospel texts we can recover the echoes of His simple, homely eloquence. His sermons were not carefully prepared, but entirely spontaneous. He taught by means of parables and stories.

But the Jews would not have listened to Jesus, or believed in Him, if He had not performed miracles. The apostle Paul, who knew both Jews and Greeks, wrote, "For the Jews require a sign, and the Greeks seek after wisdom" (*1 Cor. 1 : 22*). Jesus was compelled to perform miracles, for did He not once complain, "Except they see signs and wonders, they will not believe."

A large number of works illustrating parables, sermons, and miracles exist, but we shall here describe only a few which depict the sermons and miracles, since in the illustrations of the parables Jesus plays no active part, being simply the narrator.

THE MIRACLES

Nowadays, Christians attach more importance to Christ's teaching than to His miracles. It was the exact opposite at the time when Jesus lived and up until the sixteenth century: the change is due largely to the reformers and the humanists. The Synoptic Gospels record about twenty miracles, the Fourth Gospel only seven. It is worth noting that Jesus performed miracles to relieve human suffering or misfortune, and not with a view to publicity. Commentators divide the miracles into three classes:

1. Those connected with food or drink, e.g., at the Marriage in Cana, and in the Feeding of the Multitude.
2. The healing miracles: there are a number of these, and the diseases cured vary, e.g., blindness, paralysis, leprosy, etc.
3. Raising the dead: there are three of these, the widow's son at Nain, Jairus' daughter, and Lazarus.

No single work illustrating all the Gospel miracles has survived. However, we cannot say whether one ever existed. The oldest collection, which is incomplete, is in the abbatial church at Müstair, in Grisons, Switzerland. Another collection, also incomplete, is in the Church of Oberzell, on the Isle of Reichenau (Lake of Constance). But illustrations of individual miracles were very common, at any rate until the sixteenth century; from then on, only certain particular ones seem to have become favourites.

The turning of the water into wine, at the wedding feast at Cana in Galilee, is the first miracle recorded in the Gospels. The story is very well known and it has been a favourite subject with artists since the fourth century. The reason for its popularity was probably its symbolism. The miracle was seen as prefiguring the Holy Communion under the element of wine, while that of the Loaves and Fishes prefigured it under the element of bread. Such an interpretation of the miracle favoured a prolixity of artistic styles, which were helps to the religious instruction of the preacher. But, of course, care had to be taken not to let the picture of this miracle resemble the Last Supper, to which it might bear a superficial resemblance.

In pictures of the turning of water into wine, Jesus is usually standing in the foreground, in front of the six jars into which a servant pours water. In the middle distance, the steward of the feast is seen sampling the wine which Jesus has just had sent to him. In the background is the table with the food, and alongside it the married couple with Mary. In some cases, Mary is shown standing beside Jesus.

At the time of the Renaissance, the secularisation of art, mentioned above, affected this too. A simple wedding breakfast in a Galilean village became a sumptuous feast at which it was impossible to believe that the wine would ever run out. There is a picture by Paul Veronese in the Louvre in Paris, in which one can recognise portraits of Francis I, Charles V, Mary Stuart, Soliman the Magnificent, etc. Jesus has vanished in a crowd of guests.

After being treated with so much sumptuous detail, as is seen in the pictures of the sixteenth, seventeenth and eighteenth centuries, the theme of the miracle fell into disuse. Today it has reappeared, changed in a naïvely exotic manner, on the walls of the Anglican Cathedral at Port-au-Prince, Haiti. It is a real scene of West Indian

folk-life, with drums, rocking-chairs, and Havana cigars, but it is also a real country wedding where, judging by the number of upturned glasses, the wine might quite well have run out.

Jesus, drawn larger than the others, stands in the middle of the picture and lays His hands over the water that a servant is pouring into two jars. Jesus is shown clean-shaven, with bronzed complexion and long, dark hair. It is too early to judge whether this example of contemporary Christian art indicates a renewal of a theme of inspiration that had been spoilt in Europe.

Eucharistic symbolism accounts for the coupling of the miracle at the Marriage Feast in Cana with that of the Loaves and Fishes. The latter miracle is recorded by all the evangelists: Luke and John report one instance only, Matthew and Mark report two.

Although similar to the miracle at Cana, the multiplication of the loaves and fishes had a slightly different iconographic history. This theme was abandoned sooner, probably because the subject did not lend itself to such glamorous treatment. From the second to the sixteenth century, it was the constant subject of all artistic productions—sculpture, mosaics, miniatures, frescoes, retables, and ivories.

Jesus healed people, as well as feeding them. The healing miracles are difficult to classify, and it would be tedious to make an inventory of their artistic treatment. Even more so than with the feeding miracles, the healing ones are rarely pictured after the sixteenth century. Why was this? Probably because of people's changed views about illness and of the importance of miracles in the ministry of Jesus. In the days of Jesus, and in the Middle Ages, a sick man was primarily a man possessed of a devil—which is still believed by some primitive races. So Jesus' healings, usually by means of mere contact with His person or by imposition of His hands, struck the imagination of the people, who saw in them a fight between the forces of good and evil. This accounts for the importance attached to miracles both by the Jews of Jesus' time and by the masses during the Middle Ages.

After the sixteenth century, when views as to the nature of ill-health changed, the healing miracles came to be regarded as less important, and their artistic representation grew less frequent. Of the three raisings of the dead recorded in the Gospels, that of Lazarus was regarded as the most important, and came to oust the other two as subjects for artistic representation. Christians thought of this miracle as Christ's greatest, and a pledge of their own resurrection. This accounts for its persistent popularity as a subject of Christian art.

An interesting fact about miracles is that native art, with one or two exceptions, seldom pictures them, although it is generous in its representation of the parables.

The place of miracles in Christian art has greatly varied through the centuries for very differing reasons, sometimes artistic repletion, sometimes changes in people's beliefs. Such continuity as we find is due to a particular miracle possessing a universally acknowledged symbolism.

Christ's teaching, which is addressed to all men, is clear and simple, going straight to the heart of the matter, and illustrated by simple stories based on the everyday life of the countryside. During His public ministry, Jesus spoke sometimes to His intimates—the Apostles He had chosen—sometimes to a single questioner, and sometimes to the crowd. As the religion of Israel was not very well-disposed towards women, Jesus, in order to dissociate Himself from the ancient law, frequently conversed with them. Three of them who figure in His life are the Samaritan woman, the woman taken in adultery, and Mary Magdalene. They have not all received equal treatment in iconographic art.

We have pictures of the Samaritan woman, but the Western Church has none of the woman taken in adultery; indeed, the Gospel passage has been removed in many versions, as being a late addition. Unquestionably the most popular subject with artists is Mary Magdalene.

For a long time, the symbolism of the scene of Jesus with the Samaritan woman at Jacob's well was clearly understood. The Samaritan, being a stranger in Jewish eyes, represents the non-Jews or Gentiles who have responded to the Christian gospel. The still waters of Jacob's well, symbolising the Old Law, contrast with the living water, the sign of Christian baptism. But will Christian art continue faithful? Already we see in a picture of Indian origin such a toning-down of Jacob's well as to make the scene merely one of Jesus teaching an emotional and attentive woman.

The Gospels tell the stories of Mary Magdalene and Mary of Bethany, the sister of Martha and Lazarus. As the events occurred fairly close together, they are often confused in the artistic representation. Whenever one sees a picture of a woman seated at the feet of Jesus, one thinks immediately of Mary Magdalene, out of whom He had cast seven devils *(Mark 16 : 9, Luke 8 : 2)*. It is a fairly widely-held belief, dating from early times but not really supported by the Gospels, that Mary Magdalene and Mary, the sister of Martha, who wiped Jesus' feet, *(John 12 : 3)* are the same person, and also that she is the "woman which was a sinner," and who "stood at his feet behind him weeping, and began to wash his feet with tears, and did wipe them with the hairs of her head, and kissed his feet, and anointed them with the ointment" *(Luke 7 : 37, 38)*.

Jesus' approach to women, especially to those who had sinned, was in great contrast with the ideas of His age, and showed clearly that the spirit of love and mercy is the essence of Christianity.

In Europe, popular art made use of this theme until the nineteenth century, even though it inspired few great artists. It reappears in those countries where native art is just budding, and in this connection it is significant that, at the missionary exhibition in Rome in 1950, a large number of watercolours and paintings were shown that came from Asian countries (India, Vietnam, etc.).

Lenient as He was toward human weakness, Jesus was not less sensitive to childlike innocence. St. Matthew *(19 : 13-15)*, St. Mark *(10 : 13-16)*, and St. Luke *(18 : 15-17)* all record the occasion when Jesus said to His apostles, "Suffer little children, and forbid them not, to come unto me; for of such is the kingdom of heaven." Though little used during the Middle Ages, this subject became popular in the art of the Reformation period and nearly all the examples we have come from those countries—Holland, Northern Germany—where the Reformed religion was prevalent. Today, in the Far East, where there are many children, the subject is being developed in the paintings of the school of Peking, by Alfred Thomas in India, and in some anonymous works from New Zealand.

Two particularly important events, the triumphal Entry into Jerusalem on Palm Sunday, and the Last Supper on Maundy Thursday, are recorded in the last week of Jesus' life on earth.

The Entry into Jerusalem was solemn, joyful, and triumphant. All the Gospels report it in full *(Matthew 21 : 1-11, Mark 11 : 1-11, Luke 19 : 28-40, John 12 : 12-19)*. Jesus had just raised Lazarus from the dead and wanted to get to Jerusalem, a distance of about a mile and a quarter, in order to keep the Passover. His Apostles procured an ass and the small party set off. The fame of Jesus, enhanced by His most recent miracle, explains the ovation He received from the Jewish crowd assembled for the feast. It seemed that He really was the Messiah, the son of David.

Quite early, from the fourth century, this scene is the subject of artistic representation. In Syrian art, Jesus rides side-saddle; in the West, He rides astride, with bare feet. The latter style became common only later, half-way through the Middle Ages.

The first carvings of the subject occur on a sarcophagus in the vaults of the Vatican. Jesus appears clean-shaven, with fairly short hair. He looks like a young Roman, and this is surely a happy adaptation of the art of Imperial Rome to illustrate a Gospel scene.

During the Middle Ages, Palm Sunday was a very popular feast in Germany and its surrounding countries. Processions were organised in which a statue of Christ riding astride on an ass—either a live animal or a wooden one on wheels—was paraded through the streets from one church to another. As a special treat, children were allowed to take turns in riding pillion behind Christ; possibly as a reminder that He had said "Suffer little children, and forbid them not, to come unto me." This custom was given up at the Reformation, but the figures—those that were not destroyed—can be seen in the museums at Nuremberg, Strasbourg, Basle, Zürich, and Bolzano.

In the art of the West, there has been little change in the treatment of Christ's entry into Jerusalem. Jesus usually rides from the left to the right of the picture, with His right hand raised, blessing the people. Men and children crowd round Him, shouting and throwing their clothes on the ground before Him. In a corner, a man sitting in a tree reminds one of Zacchaeus who, being short, had climbed a sycamore tree to get a better view of Jesus as He rode through Jericho *(Luke 19: 1-10)*. Today, this subject is still used in the art of Africa (Makarere College) and China.

The Last Supper, that last and supreme occasion for intimate converse between Jesus and His apostles, has inspired many pictures designed both to edify and to interest the faithful.

To start with, Jesus washes His disciples' feet, a service normally performed by a slave just before his master sits down to his meal. Later, Jesus causes surprise and consternation by announcing that one of them will betray Him. Then, alone with His faithful friends, the Master opens His heart to them in a conversation of incomparable beauty, summing up their previous three years' training, and seeking to guide them through the years to come, and finally, as a pledge of His love, Jesus institutes the Sacrament of the Eucharist.

Pictorial art has recorded for us all three episodes—the Washing of the Feet, the Announcement of Judas's Betrayal, and the Institution of the Eucharist.

As regards the first: this is recorded in St. John's Gospel, Chapter 13: "He riseth from supper, and laid aside his garments; and took a towel, and girded himself. After that he poureth water into a bason, and began to wash the disciples' feet, and to wipe *them* with the towel wherewith he was girded." And then He sums up the implication of His act: "For I have given you an example, that ye should do as I have done to you."

In Byzantine art, Jesus stands; in Western, He kneels before St. Peter. This theme is illustrated in early Christian art since the sixth century, and today continues in Africa. These pictures had a great teaching value, showing Jesus giving His disciples a final lesson in humility, and reminding Christians of their duty to follow the example of Him whose name they bear.

The announcement by Jesus of the forthcoming betrayal has been illustrated on canvas, in stone and in wood-carving. Conflicting emotions fill the hearts of the apostles—wonder, horror, anger. It is an immensely dramatic moment, forcefully shown in the attitudes and features of the apostles, however much the details may vary in different pictures. Two apostles are always recognisable: John from his leaning on Our Lord, and Judas (painted without a halo) from his surly features and the purse which is always shown prominently.

Dramatic as is this historical event, it cannot compare in mystical fervour and meaning with the Institution of the Eucharist. For the Last Supper was more than a lesson in humility, more than a crisis reached immediately before the Passion: it was and remains for all time that moment in time when the Holy Communion was first taken, when the Sacrament was instituted. So there is a double significance: it reminds us first that Jesus instituted the Sacrament, and secondly, that Christ stands behind the priest who distributes the elements—Christ giving His body and His blood for the redemption of mankind.

As a matter of iconographic history, the above theme originates from Byzantium, where the Last Supper is represented symbolically, rather than historically or realistically. Christ, the great High Priest, communicates each apostle in turn in both the bread and the wine. Here one sees the influence of the Greek liturgy, which gives communion under both kinds. Architectural considerations helped the interpretation, as the scene was usually shown in murals, on each side of the Holy Table.

In the West, equally influenced by the liturgy, Christ is seen only once, with the host but without the chalice. This was so because in the Western Church—at least until the Reformation—communion was given only in the element of bread. After the Council of Trent this latter theme was used more than ever in Catholic countries, in opposition to the Reformers. In fact, iconography was used to illustrate theological differences.

After the sixteenth century, pictures of the Last Supper became numerous and popular. This is shown by the large number of small, framed pictures and engravings, often of little artistic merit, which it inspired. Although stereotyped, many of the pictures show great fervour and tenderness.

Christian art has been generous in its illustrations of Christ's public ministry. These pictures have evolved differently from those of the Nativity and Childhood of Jesus. The reason is plain. The scenes of Christ's early life are practically all just narrative, and the details that have supplemented the often meagre Gospel accounts are mostly picturesque tales culled from legends. They are tolerated by a Church always indulgent toward human simpleness. Illustrations of episodes in the public ministry raise quite different considerations. In effect, these are interpretations of the teaching of Jesus, as the Gospels record it. The passages chosen from the teaching, and their interpretations, reveal to us the history of the Church's life, as well as the major tendencies existing in different periods. Pictures are not meant merely to be decorative, but are also for edification and instruction. With no other aid, one could almost write a history of the Church's worship and controversies, even of the heresies.

Pictures are born, change, and sometimes even disappear for theological reasons. Again, some subjects are more popular than others, reflecting changes in religious feelings. To some people, Christ appears as Miracle-Worker, and they will seek to illustrate His miracles; to others, He is above all the Divine Teacher, and these people will portray His teaching by illustrations of His parables or sermons. At certain periods mystics will develop an allegorical style in which, searching for psychological, human reality, they will seek to produce pictures to stir men's hearts. Finally, just as there is a life for languages, so there is a dynamic for pictures: they disappear or merge in order to avoid confusion. And pictures adapt themselves to different civilizations, being born, living, and dying with them. Amidst the confusion and whims of history, one figure abides, Jesus Christ. And through the wars, conflicts, and passions of twenty centuries, and in spite of philosophical and scientific theories, all Christians, in their best moments, hear Him who said "I am the Way, the Truth and the Life."

CHRIST IN THE MIDST OF THE DOCTORS, BY VINAYAK S. MASOJI – INDIA

Jesus, seated like a Brahman, is teaching the Doctors of the Law. His completely serene air is in striking contrast with the mixed feelings of His audience. In the right background Mary and Joseph seem astonished at having found their child in such company.

If the general arrangement of the picture owes something to the European tradition, the details are Indian and the general impression is of a hybrid work, half European, half Indian.

The Gospels do not tell us specifically whether Jesus was baptised by immersion or aspersion. In the oldest pictures He goes into the waters of the Jordan up to His armpits or His waist, which is clearly baptism by immersion. But in the cupola of the baptistry of the Church of St. Vitale in Ravenna, John the Baptist makes a gesture indicative of baptism by aspersion over Christ's head. This is a combination of the two rites, and it is also found in this Chinese plate of the eighteenth century, which belongs to a series known as *Rouge de fer*. Its composition is clearly inspired by Western pictures, but one has the feeling that the Chinese artist was not really at his ease. This specimen, from the Musée Guimet in Paris, shows the conservatism of iconography. The majority of Christian churches had long since administered baptism by aspersion, but the old rite was retained when showing our Lord's baptism. However, in order to avoid confusing the faithful, who knew only the newer rite, Jesus is shown being baptised by immersion and aspersion at the same time.

THE BAPTISM OF CHRIST – CHINA

The missionaries to Asia and Africa took with them not only the artistic inheritance of the previous centuries, but also the particular styles and fashions either of their own countries or their religious orders. Therefore, no continuity existed between the local and imported artistic traditions. But these different styles and fashions have not resisted the encroachments of time. Consider this "Baptism" by an African artist. He has chosen bronze as his medium, common enoug hin Africa but rare in the West. Because baptism by immersion is practised only rarely nowadays, and the medium of sculpture is also a difficult one in which to represent immersion in the waters of the Jordan, Jesus is shown as being baptised by aspersion only. In any case, this will remind the faithful of the manner of their own baptism.

In this picture the Indian artist, Frank Wesley, has completely abandoned the traditional treatment of the Gospel story of Christ's baptism. For centuries Christian art had shown, either John actually baptising Jesus, or else Jesus humbly kneeling before the Baptist, asking for His baptism; the intervention of God the Father being symbolised by a hand or a head and shoulders coming through a cloud.

Here there is no baptism, either by immersion or aspersion; it seems already to have taken place. The Holy Spirit comes down as a dove, and the Father's voice is symbolised by the celestial brightness. John the Baptist is shown behind Jesus and following Him, in recognition that his role as "forerunner" is accomplished, while Jesus, emerging from the River Jordan, serenely assumes His role as teacher and redeemer.

THE BAPTISM OF CHRIST,
BY FRANK WESLEY — INDIA

The Temptation of Christ has inspired differently the gothic sculptor from Plaimpied, in France, and the young African painter from Makarere College. The carving is symbolical, the painting realistic. The sculptor depicts Christ's suffering, the painter His loneliness, but both seem to be in equal difficulty in portraying the devil. In the carving he appears as two monstrous beasts; in the painting as an angel, complete with horns and tail, a style that follows a popular European tradition.

Inspired by his native art, the Indian Joseph Pereira has largely followed the story of the mediation and enlightenment of the Buddha in this painting of the Temptation of Christ. It shows Christ sitting calm and serene amidst a crowd of demons.

These three portrayals of the Temptation, coming from three different continents, illustrate the potential richness of Christian art—universal as regards its sources, local only in its forms of expression.

The total number of pictures of the Marriage in Cana of Galilee shows how a religious theme can become satiated by mere prettiness and pomposity; so much so that one would have thought that this event in Our Lord's life had now ceased to inspire any artist. On the contrary, quite recently a group of simple and enthusiastic artists in Haiti have started to decorate the walls of the Cathedral of the Holy Trinity at Port-au-Prince, Haiti. using this theme. The frescoes show the Marriage at Cana as a typically West Indian wedding, with brilliant colouring, but their sincerity and inspiration are not at all affected by the overcrowded detail.

86

Illustrations of the text "Suffer little children to come unto me, and forbid them not" are comparatively recent. They were unknown in the Middle Ages, becoming popular only from the sixteenth century, especially in some of the countries where the Reformed religion prevailed (North Germany and the Low Countries). There are not, therefore, many examples, though they are often found as decorations in children's homes and orphanages. Since the beginning of this century certain painters of Asia and New Zealand have taken up this subject, the most interesting example being without question this painting on silk by Luc Tcheng, an artist well-known as the founder of a school of Christian art in Peking before the second World War.

DENOS MVNDABAT GRATES

DECEM LEPROSI

THE HEALING OF THE TEN LEPERS

THE MIRACLE OF THE BLEEDING

THE MIRACLE OF THE DROPSICAL

THE MIRACLE OF THE LOAVES AND THE FISHES — GERMANY

JESUS AND MARY MAGDELAINE
GERMANY

92

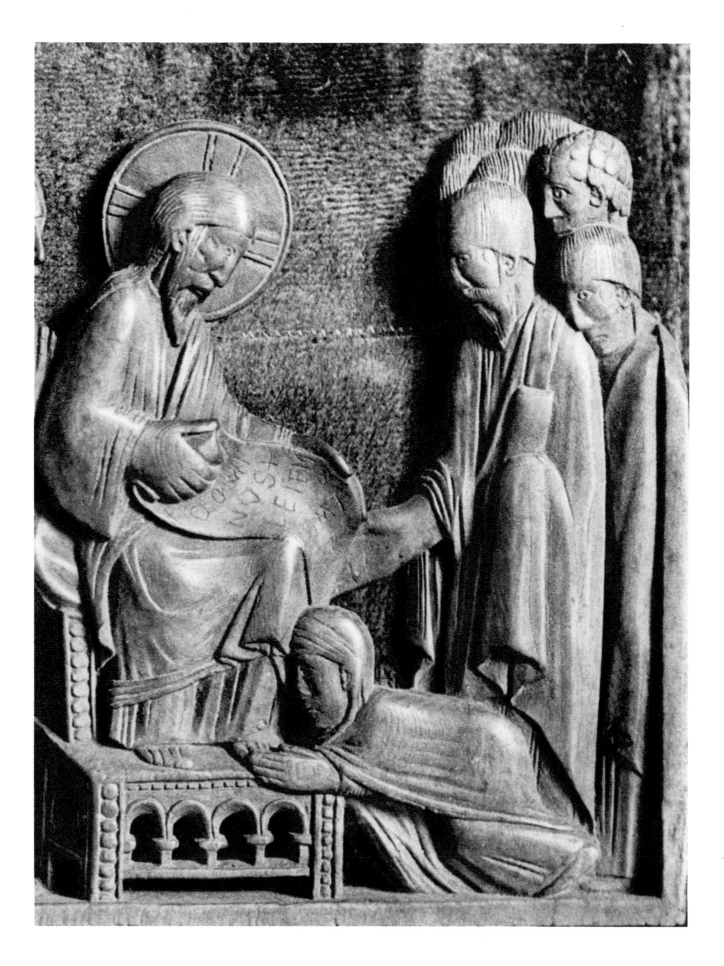

"All power is given unto me in heaven and in earth. Go ye therefore, and teach all nations, baptizing them in the name of the Father, and of the Son, and of the Holy Ghost: teaching them to observe all things whatsoever I have commanded you: and, lo, I am with you alway, even unto the end of the world." *(Matthew 28 : 18-20.)* These verses, with which St. Matthew's Gospel ends, have seldom inspired artists, who preferred more symbolical scenes, such as the Delivery of the Law to Peter and Paul, or else texts with a more precise meaning, such as the Promise of the Keys to St. Peter. So a modern artist who wishes to illustrate these verses will not be cramped by existing styles or modes of treatment.

Perhaps that is why this picture, by an Annamite artist, while faithful to the simplicity of the text, suggests so forcibly the dynamic commission given by Christ to the apostles, and indeed to all who pray daily to their heavenly Father "Hallowed be thy name, thy kingdom come."

96

THE ENTRY INTO JERUSALEM — EARLY CHRISTIAN SARCOPHAGUS

This Entry into Jerusalem shows the detail of the front of a Christian sarcophagus of the fourth century. It is one of, if not actually the first illustration of this episode in the life of Jesus. The influence of Roman art is clear: the folds in the togas; the hair curled in Roman fashion; and the expressions on the faces, which call to mind other reliefs of purely secular subjects. What seems outstandingly Christian is the sense of triumphant movement, as if the artist enjoyed sculpting a scene of both the Entry into Jerusalem and the triumph of the Church, then just ceasing to have to hide in the catacombs.

The style of this relief will be found in all churches of the West. In the East there is a slightly different one, inherited from the Syrian tradition, in which Christ has long hair, a beard, and rides the ass, not astride, but side-saddle, as if mounted on a throne.

This painted wooden panel used to form part of an altar built in Germany during the fourteenth century. Comparing it with the early Christian work, similarities as well as differences at once become apparent. The general composition is the same, in spite of the ten centuries between these works, which shows the strength of iconographic tradition. There are, however, some differences: the figure of Christ follows the tradition of the West of the Middle Ages, for He is bearded and with long hair. The Romans—children and adults—have been superseded by old people, and Zacchaeus, sitting in his tree, wears contemporary clothes.

In spite of a superficial similarity, these two works typify two different civilizations, a difference which is seen in the pictures we have shown which originate from Europe and those which come to us from Asia and Africa. It is the particular duty of Christian art to convey, in forms suitable to succeeding generations, the Gospel message of love, addressed to all men in all times.

On the night before His death, Jesus and the Twelve had assembled to eat the Passover. For the last time before the day which was to end His earthly ministry, He was conversing with His apostles. This miniature, taken from a Syriac Gospel now in the British Museum, shows Jesus and the apostles standing about a round table. The artist has had some difficulty in getting so many people round the table, but, in spite of the clumsiness of the drawing, the wide-open eyes and outstretched hands give a certain touching piety to this miniature.

THE LAST SUPPER — SYRIAC GOSPEL   THE LAST SUPPER — FRANCE

100

This sculptured representation of the Eucharist, which comes from French Canada, shows all the roughness of a rustic art, the characters being thick-set workers of the land. Also, the artist seems to have had difficulty in getting all the Twelve round the table, and to give greater presence to Jesus he has made Him slightly larger than the apostles.

Over the page is an example of a period when the development of art had reached its highest, and it is in striking contrast with the Canadian peasant's work. The perfection of this Eucharist, by Riemenschneider, makes it one of the highlights of Gothic wood-carving.

But the important contrast is that the Canadian work reminds the faithful of the institution of the Holy Communion, while the German shows rather the astonishment of the apostles when told that one of them will betray their Master. The German master has illustrated a detail of the scene, the Canadian rustic its inner meaning.

THE LAST SUPPER
BY RIEMENSCHNEIDER
GERMANY

105

THE PASSION

Historically, the death of Jesus on the Cross is probably the best-attested event of His life. In addition to the witness of all the Gospels, the great Latin historian, Tacitus, who was not a Christian, mentions it *(Annals, XV)*. But the death of Jesus is much more than just an event in history: it is the very corner-stone of Christianity. As Paul wrote to his Christian converts at Corinth, "For I determined not to know anything among you, save Jesus Christ, and him crucified" *(I Cor. 2 : 2)*.

Shortly before the Crucifixion, Jesus endured many moments of suffering, of which the first recorded was the Agony in the Garden of Gethsemane. There He fought the natural human dread of suffering and death, which He knew to be the price of accepting His Father's will. He conquered His fears, and thereby secured man's redemption. The sixth-century mosaics at Ravenna illustrate this scene, but as it is essentially a sad one, it did not become popular until the fifteenth century, after which Southern Germany and Alsace produced some picturesque and moving groups of the Agony in the Garden. Jesus is shown sometimes prostrate on the ground, sometimes kneeling, and sometimes, especially in the later works, seated. An angel from heaven presents Him either with the instruments of His passion, or with a chalice.

As the Agony in the Garden is described in all the Synoptic Gospels, it will most probably inspire future Asian or African artists, who will doubtless depict the garden as one of their own country. Equally, Jesus and the angel will be Chinese, Indian, or African. We have an example of such a development in a picture by the Chinese artist, George Wang.

Another dramatic event which took place in the Garden of Gethsemane was the arrest of Jesus. As this scene is very rarely depicted in the contemporary art either of Europe or the missionary countries, it will not be irrelevant to consider it in a little detail.

The Arrest presents the artist with a choice of moments to illustrate. First, there is the bargain between Judas and the High Priest; then the kiss whereby Judas identified Jesus to the soldiers; and, finally, His actual arrest. In Byzantine art, there is a great difference between that of the Imperial Court and that of the monasteries. The former, very conscious of God's majesty, has not really illustrated scenes of the Passion, whereas the latter treats them in great detail. Examples are the frescoes in the Protaton of Vatopedi, in Mount Athos. In their treatment of this subject, Roman, and later Gothic art, follow their own individual styles. At the end of the Middle Ages these scenes are presented with a realism calculated to stir the emotions of the faithful.

Although appearing through the sixteenth, seventeenth and to a slight extent in the eighteenth centuries, few examples of the Arrest are found in any contemporary art, either European or non-European.

Once arrested, Jesus was taken in turn before the Jewish and Roman authorities. The Jewish Sanhedrin found Him guilty of blasphemy in claiming to be the Son of God: before Pilate He was accused of sedition for having posed as the King of the Jews.

The different appearances before Caiaphas, the High Priest, Annas, Caiaphas' father-in-law, Pilate, the Roman Governor, and Herod Antipas, the tetrarch of Galilee, are somewhat confused in the Gospel narratives, and do not make suitable iconographic subjects.

Three of the most striking moments have, however, been seized upon by artists, *viz.*, Pilate's Condemnation of Jesus, the Scourging of Jesus, and Pilate's Presentation of Jesus to the Crowd. *(John 19.)*

The Condemnation of Jesus was an early subject of Christian art. It is seen on the sarcophagi in the Vatican Grottoes, on the door of the Church of St. Sabina in Rome, and in a mosaic in the Church of S. Apollinare Nuovo, in Ravenna. But this subject became even more popular after the spread of the devotion of the Stations of the Cross, of which the appearance of Christ before Pilate is the first. This extremely popular Roman Catholic devotion appeared at the end of the Middle Ages, under the influence of the Franciscans, who were the guardians of the Holy Places. The number of these pictures—or "Stations"—was originally seven; its present number, fourteen, dates from the seventeenth century. These Stations are designed for devotional purposes, and depict incidents in Christ's journey from Pilate's house to His entombment: they are based on texts from both the Canonical and Apocryphal Gospels, and also on the mystical writings of St. Bonaventure and St. Bridget of Sweden.

In country churches, these Stations of the Cross often possess a simplicity of feeling more emotionally moving than those in large city churches, which are often just copies of old masters.

It is almost certain that Asian and African artists will produce pictures or carvings of the Stations of the Cross for their churches. Indeed there are already some examples of this in Africa, where the works show great religious feeling.

Even before the development of the Stations of the Cross, Christians had been deeply affected by certain details of the Passion—the Scourging, the Crowning with Thorns, and the Presentation of Jesus to the Crowd.

Although the Scourging is mentioned very briefly in the Gospels, it has been prolifically illustrated ever since the Roman period. The beautiful panels at Verona and Novgorod are well known. Like all the iconography of the Passion, the pictures of this scene became more and more realistic at the end of the Middle Ages. For example, in the fifteenth-century works hardly a square inch of Jesus' body has escaped the lash, which the executioners wield with quite revolting fury.

After being scourged, Jesus had a crown of thorns placed on His head. Again this was a favourite subject, and very many pictures of it existed at the end of the Middle Ages. Jesus is usually shown sitting, and His look of sorrowful resignation is in striking contrast with the angry looks and gestures of His executioners.

The third episode, the Presentation of Jesus to the Crowd, sometimes known as "Ecce Homo," is typically Western, being unknown in early Christian and Byzantine art, and appearing in the West only shortly before the Reformation. Its great popularity has extended as far as modern Poland. In all its realistic details, Jesus looks a pitiable subject of Jewish bear-baiting. But to Christians He remains the Man of Sorrows suffering for the redemption of mankind.

By the Roman law, those condemned to death by crucifixion had to carry their own cross to the place of execution. According to the Fourth Gospel this took place, but the other three synoptists say that the soldiers compelled one Simon, of Cyrene, in Africa, to carry the Cross for Jesus.

Byzantine art follows the account of the Synoptic Gospels: Simon carries the Cross, and Jesus follows him, with a rope round His neck. In the West, Jesus is shown carrying His Cross, though sometimes helped by Simon. Although the Byzantine pictures are somewhat coldly narrative, those of the West have a dramatic and emotional quality.

According to the devotion of the Stations of the Cross, Christ's last journey to Calvary was marked by certain incidents: Jesus' three falls; His meeting with His mother; the wiping of His face by Veronica; and His meeting with the "daughters of Jerusalem," to whom He said: "Weep not for me, but weep for yourselves and for your children" *(Luke 23: 28)*.

Having arrived at the place of execution, the soldiers stripped Jesus of His garments and nailed Him to the Cross, which they fixed firmly in the ground. The details of the Crucifixion have been portrayed since the Middle Ages, but the one essential is the Cross, standing between earth and heaven, on which hangs Jesus, dying for the redemption of the world, having perfectly fulfilled His Father's will.

Paradoxically, the earliest known picture of Christ Crucified is also a horrible caricature—the Palatine Crucifixion. In 1856, Carucci discovered a *graffito* on a wall in the pages' chamber of the Imperial Palace on the Palatine Hill. It is devoid of any artistic merit, and shows a cross, on which a man stands upright, with arms flung wide apart. But the man has an ass's head. In the left foreground of this grotesque crucifix there is a much smaller man, in an adoring posture, and a Greek inscription reads "Alaxamene worships his God." A fine answer to such blasphemy! And next door there is an inscription "Faithful Alaxamene."

In the third century, a Christian could hardly show a picture of Christ on the Cross in public. Such an act would have been provocative of scandal and blasphemy: so they chose other means of showing forth God's love of man. Primitive Christian art disliked featuring Christ as having died ignominiously between two wrongdoers. So, in the catacombs, we find that His sacrifice is always presented under the theme of the lamb. And hence the first Cross, set up by Constantine and Helena, bore no effigy of Christ. But from the fifth century onwards, Jesus was portrayed on the Cross between two thieves.

The Quinisext Council (Trullan Synod) in A.D. 692 approved this development on theological grounds. The danger of a merely symbolical representation of the Crucified Jesus was that it might encourage the monophysite heresy. This heresy denied the catholic doctrine that in Christ's person two natures existed, divine and human, and asserted that only divine existed in His person, and so regarded the Sacrifice on Calvary as purely symbolical. The Fathers of the Council sought to counteract this danger by encouraging an artistic development that was just beginning, and ordered that painters should show "Jesus living, suffering, and dying in the flesh for the redemption of the world."

From the sixth to the eleventh centuries, Crucifixes show a living, triumphant Christ, with eyes wide open: a man indeed, but also God. The same idea underlies the following passage from St. Chrysostom (A.D. c. 347-407), written, of course, long before the Quinisext Council.

"See how, even on the Cross, He accomplished all without trouble; confiding His mother to the care of the beloved disciple, fulfilling the prophecies, and giving hope to the thief. And yet, before He was crucified, fear and horror covered Him in sweat. What had happened? The answer is clear: there we see natural human weakness, here, the fullness of power. Since He is almighty, the end came when He willed it, and He willed it after He had finished all His work . . . It was not after He had died that His head fell forward, as happens to us men; but that when He let His head fall forward, then He died. And so the Gospel shows Him to have been supreme over all things." (Quoted in Millet, *Iconographie de l'Evangile*, p. 396.)

The Crucifixes of this long period—sixth to eleventh centuries—although they had much in common, can be divided into two distinct types.

The largest number originated from, or are under the influence of, Syrian art. In these, Christ is bearded, of ripe age, and always clothed in a long, sleeveless tunic, called a "colobium." The oldest example is the famous miniature of the monk Rabula (A.D. 586). The devotion to St. Voult of Lucca popularised this style, and the Roman Crucifixes, especially those in Catalonia, are probably the last examples of this manner of portraying Jesus on the Cross.

But another style of Crucifix existed, though these were less common. These showed Jesus as a young man, beardless, and wearing only a narrow loin-cloth. His hands and feet are not always nailed to the Cross, and His arms are flung wide open as if praying.

There exist some rudimentary examples in some very old works in jasper and cornelian. Two others which are well known are the ivory now in the British Museum, and the panel in the door of the Church of St. Sabina, Rome. Both are believed to be fifth century. These Crucifixes are more symbolical or mystical than realistic. The suffering and the triumph are clearly apparent. Jesus' body remains straight, and His chest, head, and arms are in a physically impossible position. Often too, a royal diadem adorns His head.

From the eleventh century a great change took place. The Christ of Roman art, as straight upon His Cross as on a throne, gradually disappears to give place to a dead Christ, with closed eyes and head limp on His shoulder, an object of terrible pity. This change, which occurred almost simultaneously throughout the West, is seen first in works coming from the Rhineland. Some explanation of such a change seems called for, but it is not altogether easy. One view is that, under Byzantine influence, theologians sanctioned this change because Christ's death was not the result of a normal physical process, but of an act of His divine will.

Others give the simpler explanation that it is due to a very great increase in sensitivity, particularly religious sensitivity, which went on right up to the end of the Middle Ages. Francis of Assisi, Bridget of Sweden, the

INRI

O CRUX
AVE

A CHARTRES. CHEZ GARNIER-ALLABRE.

meditations of the pseudo-Bonaventure, and the Benedictine influence, all had the same object: to direct the devotions of the faithful toward Christ's humanity, and to stir up the emotions by descriptions of His sufferings. In her *Revelations*, Bridget of Sweden (d. A.D. 1373) tells of a vision she had in which Mary, the mother of Jesus, described her Son's death. The terrifying realism of the description must have inspired many an artist of the fourteenth and fifteenth centuries:

"When my Son," said Mary, "saw me standing with His friends at the foot of the Cross, He cried out to His Father in a loud distressed voice, 'My Father, why hast thou forsaken me?' As if He said 'Only you, my Father, can now take pity on me.' Then His eyes became half-dead, His teeth covered in blood, His face drawn, His mouth open, and His tongue dripping blood. So dried up was His body, that His chest seemed glued to His back, as if He had no entrails. All the rest was pale from the immense loss of blood. His hands and feet were fixed stiffly on the Cross. His beard and hair were full of blood. . . . With the approach of death the immense pain broke my Son's heart. His limbs contracted and His head was slightly raised and then fell back. Through His open mouth you could see the tongue red with blood. His hands tore themselves away a little from their nails so that all His weight was on the feet. His fingers and arms became distended and His back pressed firmly against the Cross." *(Revelationum, Lib. I, cap. X, Rome, 1628.)*

Without any doubt, the above must be connected with the retable at Isenheim, where Grünewald painted a Christ who was not only dead, but already in a state of putrefaction. The sole purpose of these realistic Crucifixes is to stir our emotions, by presenting to us a picture of the Man Jesus, leaving us free to realise, if we be so minded, that this same man is the Son of God, the Saviour of the World.

A new change took place at the time of the Renaissance. An artistic Christ took the place of the wounded, tortured man. Now, paintings and carvings became anatomical studies of a perfect, beautiful, human body, a real artistic treat. Special attention was paid to Jesus' head, to which each artist gave the impress of his individuality. However, it is a pity that so languishing a Christ as that painted by Guido Reni should have become popular enough to start quite a fashion in that line.

With the invention of printing, the demand for religious pictures and Crucifixes, till then restricted more or less to corporate bodies—churches, monasteries, etc.—began to spread to individuals. An enormous number of paintings and carvings, as well as small pictures and engravings, found their way among all classes of society. Some had artistic merit and became owned either by connoisseurs, by collectors, or museums. Others, of little or no merit artistically, but often touching in their simplicity, became the property of the masses. To them, Christ on the Cross was primarily an object of devotion: the visible sign of God's love for man.

In different countries and at different times the almost magical efficacy which has been—and to a large degree is still—attributed to them is due to inherited psychological tendencies, and not to the teaching of the Church; but it does explain why some churches have stressed that only in the texts of the Gospels is the true Christ found. The death of Jesus is portrayed in a number of different forms, and it is convenient to explain certain terms used.

A *Cross* has on it no effigy of our Lord; its use is purely symbolic.

A *Crucifix* is a Cross to which an effigy of Christ Crucified is affixed.

A *Crucifixion* is a work, usually painted, showing either Jesus being nailed to the Cross by the soldiers, or else the soldiers setting up the Cross on Golgotha.

A *Calvary* is a Crucifix surrounded by one or more persons. There are those with two persons (Jesus and Mary); with three persons (Jesus, Mary, and John the Evangelist); with four persons (Jesus, Mary, John, and Mary Magdalene); or with even more, as in the Calvarys from Brittany.

So we see in the iconography of Christ on the Cross two quite distinct and not wholly consistent trends. The one emphasises the divinity of Christ, and finds its expression in idealistic, almost mystical Crucifixes and Calvarys. The other lays stress on Christ's humanity, and its art is more realistic. These trends fluctuate with the times, following what are thought to be the instructional or devotional needs of the faithful. Up to the present day the two trends have seldom been found to co-exist in any one country.

The Descent from the Cross has no place in the liturgy of the Church, which probably explains why it did not become a subject for artistic representation until about the ninth century. Some illuminated Greek manuscripts show that it originated in Byzantium, although Western picture-makers dramatised the scene by bringing into it Mary, the mother of Jesus, and John the Evangelist. Towards the end of the Middle Ages, the influence either of the mystics or the Mystery Plays added further to the scene; besides the people mentioned in the Gospels—Joseph of Arimathea and Nicodemus—not only Mary and John, but Mary Magdalene, in tears at Jesus' feet, and also two men who help Joseph and Nicodemus in their sad task.

The style reached its climax in the baroque of Flanders in the seventeenth century, where mere technical skill took the place of any real feeling. The Descent from the Cross became a well-drilled showpiece, without religious feeling.

In one Descent from the Cross, Jesus is shown at the actual moment when His limbs are being loosed from the Cross: His body is still upright, and one arm, from which the nail has been taken, hangs limp, and is supported by Mary.

In a Deposition, Jesus lies full-length at the foot of the Cross. This scene is rare, being a transitional one. Soon we find others grouped round the body of Jesus: the weeping Mary holds His head, while Mary Magdalene is at His feet. John the Evangelist supports Mary in accordance with Jesus' dying request to him. Joseph of Arimathea and Nicodemus, if present, have been pushed into the background. This scene, completely devoid of all scriptural basis, was unknown to the art of earlier centuries, but passed from Byzantium to Italy in the fourteenth century and thence to the countries of Northern Europe.

A group consisting of just the body of Jesus in the arms of His mother is a "Pietà," and became very popular because of its simplicity. Occasionally Christ's dead body is seen alone, laid out, but these works are usually excuses for exercises in anatomical study rather than for religious pictures. These pictures were given up at the Renaissance, although Rembrandt used them as a model for his "Anatomy Lesson."

According to the fourth Gospel, when Jesus was seen to be dead, Joseph of Arimathea and Nicodemus "took the body of Jesus, and wound it in linen clothes with the spices, as the manner of the Jews is to bury. Now in the place where he was crucified there was a garden; and in the garden a new sepulchre, wherein was never man yet laid. There laid they Jesus." *(John 19 : 40-42.)*

Artistic imagination has sought to add details to the above very brief statement. The scene was depicted in Byzantine monastic art, but its treatment became more realistic and moving in the West. A popular form was a sculpted group, in which seven persons were usually shown round the dead body of Jesus; namely Mary and John the Evangelist, Mary Magdalene with the two other holy women, and Joseph and Nicodemus, acting as undertakers. These "Sepulchres," to give them their contemporary name, were greatly popularised, especially in France, by the Confraternities of the Holy Sepulchre and the Franciscans. At the end of the fifteenth century, these Sepulchres became living groups in the form of funeral processions in which one can see the influence of the medieval Passion Plays. The Council of Trent sought to stop these shows, which were replaced by a new theme, based on the Christ of the Mass of St. Gregory. It was not really so new, as it derived from a Byzantine icon that had been given by Pope Gregory the Great to the Church of Santa Croce in Gerusalemme in Rome. Our Lord, with the marks of the nails and spear in His hands and His side, is half out of a sarcophagus placed on the altar. In some cases He sits on the edge of the tomb, supported by two weeping angels. This theme, prevalent, especially in France and Italy, was one result of the puritanism that followed on the Council of Trent.

Since the sixteenth century then there has been little inspiration in religious art, which has made the great mistake of trying to ape the masterpieces of secular art.

From this long account of the iconography of Our Lord's Passion, it will be seen that, although some subjects have only an ephemeral life, others have lasted uninterrupted from the end of the Roman Empire until today. The principal moments of the Passion recorded in the Gospels are the Agony in the Garden of Gethsemane; Pilate's Condemnation of Jesus; the Crowning with Thorns; Jesus' Carrying of His Cross; and the Crucifixion itself. In the eleventh century another group of themes became popular, but lasted for a short time only: the pictures of a suffering and pitiable Christ; the Ecce Homo; the Crucifixion; the Deposition; and the weeping women at His entombment.

During the first period, from the earliest times until half-way through the Middle Ages, Christian iconography was narrative or symbolical. It sought to represent with dignity the divine and human aspects of the Passion of the Son of God.

The second period, covering roughly the second half of the Middle Ages, produced works highly realistic and full of pathos, which worked on the emotions. However, these studies were spoilt by unnecessary and often ridiculous details.

The third period was influenced by the Reformation, the Counter-Reformation, and Humanism. This produced works of supreme artistic merit, but of little religious feeling.

The present is a period of transition and change, when all values, including Christian values, are questioned. For Christian art, too, the times are critical. Will the Orthodox Churches remain faithful to their traditional art, or the West resist the temptation to follow blindly in the wake of modern art? Again, in the mission countries, shall we see artistic developments comparable with those that produced the Byzantine, the Roman, and the Gothic styles?

To such questions there is but one answer. If and when a living faith and active charity have united the human family around the throne of the Father of Heaven, there will arise conditions favourable to the appearance of Christian art. Then, each Christian artist, in his own style and using his own idioms, will set forth the universal Gospel message, that the incarnate Son of God gave His life as ransom for mankind, leaving them the great commandment, "Little children . . . A new commandment I give unto you, That ye love one another; as I have loved you, that ye also love one another." *(John 13 : 33, 34.)*

The interest—and beauty—of this Chinese picture lies in its interpretation of the mind of the artist rather than in the mere portrayal of the actors. The drama of the Agony in the Garden is enhanced by the wild country, the thorny and dried up tree, and the resigned expression on the face of Jesus. The artist, George Wang, has departed from European models and portrayed Jesus and the apostles as Orientals. The angel is a young Chinese girl, unlike European angels which are always depicted as men. The Chinese, who are not fond of the realistic pictures of the West, which they think too extreme, prefer a style at once aristocratic and popular, combining deep spirituality with refined elegance.

The soldiers have entered the Garden of Gethsemane and arrested Jesus; the scene depicted by this bronze relief, one of the magnificent reliefs on the doors of the Church of San Zeno Maggiore, Verona. Like the Jews in the Middle Ages, the soldiers wear pointed hats as marks of identification. The relief has an educative value, the artist clearly wishing to contrast the shame of mere brute force with the true greatness of the Redeemer. The touching simplicity of this relief makes it a striking example of the Romanesque art of Italy.

CHRIST BEFORE PILATE — WEST AFRICA

120

CHRIST SCOURGED AT THE PILLAR — RUSSIA

A short passage from the Gospels—none of which say that Jesus was tied to a pillar—has given rise to very many artistic representations of the scourging of Christ. The relief shown opposite is in the Cathedral at Novogrod, and a similar one is on the door of the Church of San Zeno Maggiore, Verona. Christ, bound to a pillar, turns round as if to assure us that it is He Himself, and this slight movement of the head adds enormously to the emotionalism of the scene. After the Romanesque period these developed, like all those of the Passion, in a more and more realistic way. German art of the fifteenth century and the Baroque style of Italy left nothing to the imagination and had no consideration for the viewers' nerves. Such exaggerations killed this theme as a subject of inspiration, and we seldom find it in the Christian art of Asia or Africa.

This Station of the Cross has been at St. Gabriel's Mission, California, since about 1779. It was painted on coarse canvas by Indians, taught by Spanish missionaries, who, however, left great freedom of expression to their pupils. The composition may show traces of European influence, but the Indian artists have more than succeeded in expressing, rather as do children's drawings, the overbearing attitude of the soldiers, the sorrow of the "daughters of Jerusalem", and the distress of Jesus on the road to Calvary.

JESUS CARRYING HIS CROSS – USA

124

JESUS CARRYING HIS CROSS,
BY FÉLICIEN HOUNDONJI — WEST AFRICA

This small statue of Jesus carrying His Cross comes from Africa, and marks a very definite departure from the traditional iconography of the Mediterranean basin. What first surprises Westerners is its general style. Europeans have nearly always pictured Jesus carrying His Cross on one shoulder, which seems to them the natural way. Here Jesus carries the Cross on His back, His two arms curved round the arms of the Cross; tired out, He has let go the burden and is about to fall.

Another unusual detail is Jesus' clothes. He no longer wears the "coat without seam," but a garment half-Roman, half-African, and oddly enough He wears a head-dress. The African sculptor has produced a most expressive work— consider the elongation of the neck, and the position of the legs and feet. And no unnecessary ornamentation spoils the simplicity and restraint of the lines. This beautiful work appeals to African Christians, both religiously and artistically, more than any sculpture imported from Europe.

The style of this Crucifixion from West Africa is very local. Although it is far from attaining the perfection of the pagan works of art of Bénin, its common parentage is clear. One finds the same economy of method and the same emphasis on symbolism rather than emotionalism. There is also the same clumsiness in the grouping and stylisation of ornamental details.

But this Crucifixion also shows another parentage, going back even farther, for this Christ, although an African, resembles all the Christs whom for long centuries Christianity alone knew, a mystical Christ, standing on His Cross, with open eyes, triumphing over suffering and death.

THE CRUCIFIXION — WEST AFRICA

THE CRUCIFIXION — EARLY CHRISTIAN IVORY

The first six centuries of the Christian era have left us very few pictures of the Crucifixion. Christians seem to have been unwilling to allow such pictures, of what for them was above all a sign of triumph, to become an object of derision by pagans. Possibly the earliest and best preserved examples are two Calvarys. The first was probably part of the lid of a casket or reliquary. Christ is shown beardless, His head held high, and looking straight in front of Him. His hands alone are nailed to the Cross. On the right one sees Judas, hanging from a tree, while the money, price of his betrayal of Christ, is lying at his feet. This ivory probably dates from the fifth century, and is of Alexandrine origin. The sixth century Gospel of Rabula contains a Calvary painted in the Syriac style. Christ is bearded and wears long hair, and He is nailed to the Cross by His feet as well as His hands. Unlike the British Museum ivory, which shows Him naked, Christ is clothed in a long sleeveless tunic called a colobium. In each Christ is seen to be alive, His eyes open, and triumphing in spite of His sufferings.

On the occasion of the building of the Church of Saint John, Monza, Pope Gregory the Great (who reigned from 3 September 590 until 12 March 604) sent a magnificent present to Queen Theodolinda of the Lombards, who had founded the Church. There remains of this gift an inventory and sixteen ampullae containing relics, the latter being well-known as valuable sources of Christian archaeology. The ampulla shown opposite illustrates how the early Christians depicted the Crucified Jesus: a Cross surmounted by the Holy Face and placed between two thieves. Although they no longer hesitated to show His Passion, Christians still felt a repugnance to putting Jesus actually on a Cross. And to emphasize the miracle, underneath the Crucified Lord is shown risen. One sees the open tomb, which an angel and the two Marys find empty.

This work is one of the first to show Jesus on the Cross.

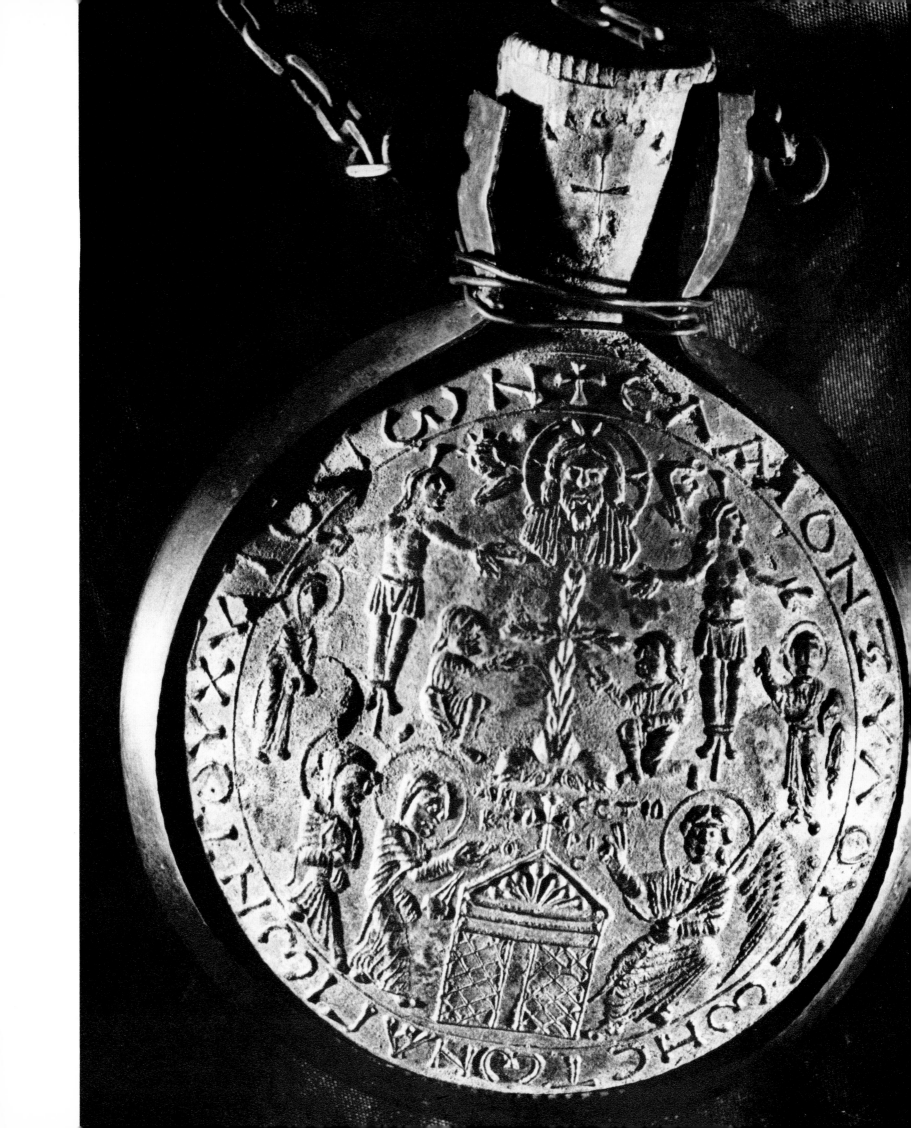

THE CRUCIFIXION — YUGOSLAVIA   THE CRUCIFIXION — BARCELONA

This one-figure Calvary is in the Church of Saint Donat, Zadar, in Yugoslavia. Christ is framed between the Sun and the Moon, a feature for which no archaeologist has been able to suggest a satisfactory explanation; whether this is a pagan survival, a lost symbolism, or a supposed beauty. The theme originates in the East, probably Syria, where it is frequently found among ancient monuments. Its original meaning has been lost, and it may well be that it will not again figure in Christian art.

The first Christians disliked making pictures of the Cross, but they were not slow to notice how birds spread their wings in the form of one, while their chirpings sounded almost like a prayer *(Tertullian, de Oratione, 39)*. This unusual Crucifix, which comes from far-off Brazil, brings the same thought to our minds.

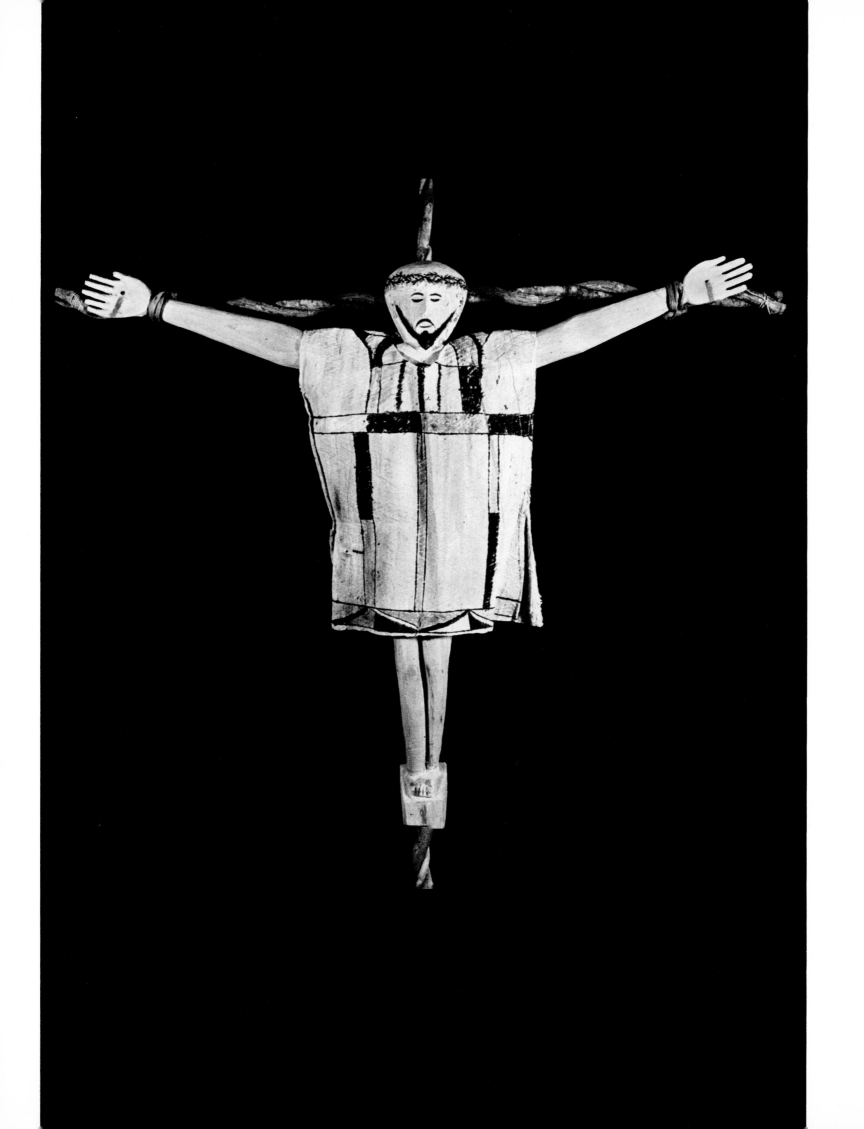

THE CRUCIFIXION — DENMARK

THE CRUCIFIXION, BY TRIVIKRAM — INDIA

THE CRUCIFIXION — TANGANYIKA

THE CRUCIFIXION – AFRICA

Hymn to Christ

"Let your bearing towards one another arise out of
your life in Christ Jesus.
For the divine nature was His from the first;
yet He did not think to snatch at equality with God,
but made Himself nothing, assuming the nature of a slave.
Bearing the human likeness, revealed in human shape,
He humbled Himself, and in obedience accepted even death
—death on a cross.
Therefore God raised Him to the heights and bestowed
on Him the name above all names, that at the name of
Jesus every knee should bow—in heaven, on earth,
and in the depths—and every tongue confess, 'Jesus
Christ is Lord,' to the glory of God the Father."

(Philippians 2:5-11 [The New English Bible].)

140

From the time of the fifth century, Christians have been used to seeing Jesus pictured on the Cross. Both the Crucifix and the unadorned Cross express a belief common to practically all Christians. In particular, Europe of the Middle Ages has left us a large number of representations of the Crucified Christ, some carved in precious metals or in ivory, some illuminated on parchment or graven in stone in cathedrals. None, however, express popular piety more than the wooden carvings, which are often the only adornment of country churches. There the Christ is the protector of the church—itself a sanctuary. He is the Christ not only of the Church Universal, but of their parish in particular.

CHRIST — SPAIN

Christian art has only rarely depicted Christ's burial or Christ lying outstretched. But from the fifteenth and sixteenth centuries, influenced by the confraternities of the Holy Sepulchre and by the Franciscans, then guardians of the Holy Places, many churches began to want some chapel or other spot dedicated to the memory of Christ's burial. In big churches this took the form of elaborate monumental groupings around Jesus of the Virgin, John, Mary Magdalene, Joseph of Arimathaea and Nicodemus: and often two other holy women. In smaller churches a dead Christ, usually carved in polychrome wood, was placed in a coffin. The lid was half-open, so that in the dim light the faithful could gaze upon the figure of Him who had died for their redemption.

146

Any artist trying to depict Christ, whether in painting or sculpture, faces a difficult task. How can human features be made to suggest the divine? How to picture God, made Man, who died and rose again, or convey that love which moved Christ to give His life for man? In truth the very best pictures have been—and always will be—but rough sketches, and with them we must be content. And yet even in the humblest and most anonymous of these portraits, there seems to be reflected in the face of the Man of Sorrows something of God's great love. What was beyond the resources of technical skill was provided out of the depth of the artist's own faith.

THE DEAD CHRIST — SWITZERLAND

CHRIST IN GLORY

"Now from the sixth hour there was darkness over all the land unto the ninth hour. . . . The earth did quake, and the rocks rent; And the graves were opened; and many bodies of the saints which slept, arose." *(Matthew 27 : 45, 51-52.)*

In spite of these marvels, the death of Jesus might have been nothing but a judicial error, in which case the Sanhedrin had been right, as He was only an agitator and impostor. Soon order would be restored, and the Jews could look forward to the coming of the true Messiah, who would bring to Israel her freedom.

The Jewish leaders, however, did not feel quite happy, so they went and asked Pilate's help to prevent the possibility that Jesus' disciples would try to remove the corpse and claim that He had risen. Pilate again declined to take responsibility, telling them "Ye have a watch: go your way, make *it* as sure as ye can" *(Matthew 27 : 65)*, which they did.

Only the Resurrection could prove conclusively the Godhead of Him who, born in a poor home, had suffered a criminal's death. And only a firm faith in the Resurrection could have made of the frightened disciples the fearless apostles of a new, living religion that was to transform the world.

What took place between Good Friday evening and the first glorious Easter morning? The Gospels are silent on the subject, but the Apostles' Creed affirms that Jesus Christ "descended into Hell."

Hugh of St. Victor (c. A.D. 1096-1141) thus summarises the Church's belief: "When Christ died, His soul became separated from His body. His soul did not descend to the Hell of the damned, nor to the Limbo of children who die without baptism, but only to the Limbo in which dwell the souls of the Patriarchs of the Old Covenant."

The great difficulty of representing in art the descent of the soul and not the body of Jesus led artists to anticipate events and portray a risen Christ descending into Hell. So, in the Byzantine and Greek Church, the Descent into Hell takes the place of the Resurrection, it being the risen Christ who goes down. In the West, for several centuries the Descent into Hell and the Resurrection were treated independently of each other.

In primitive Byzantine pictures, Jesus tramples underfoot the overturned gates of Hell, crushes Satan with the standard of the Cross, and brings away with Him Adam and the saints of the Old Covenant. The composition of these is far from simple, as it is difficult to depict simultaneously the victory over Satan and the freeing of the saints. There are many variations on this theme.

After enjoying a measure of popularity both in the East and West, this theme was given up after the sixteenth century in favour of showing the Gospels' account of the Resurrection, namely the finding of the empty tomb and the appearance of the risen Christ, which are far too important to be ignored in Christian art. For a long time the Resurrection, like the Crucifixion, was treated symbolically. On the top of a sarcophagus in the Lateran Museum, the monogram of Christ is entwined in a crown, below which sit two guards, one awake, the other asleep.

Later medieval symbolism made use of Biblical characters: Jonah coming out of the whale's belly after three days; Samson carrying on his shoulders the gates of the city of Gaza. Other symbols were taken from the then very popular fables: the phoenix rising from his ashes; the pelican who feeds her young with her own blood from her gaping breast; the lion roaring to rouse his cubs. This method showed that the artists were rather perplexed as to how to illustrate an event of which there were no witnesses. They had recourse to treating it allusively, by showing the women's discovery of the empty tomb. Very early in the morning of the first day of the week, Mary Magdalene, and Mary, the mother of James, and Salome, came to the sepulchre with sweet spices, to complete the anointing of Jesus' body. They found the stone that had guarded the door, rolled away and the sepulchre empty. An angel, in some cases two angels, met the women at the entrance to the sepulchre. Sometimes the scene also showed the meeting of Jesus with Mary Magdalene, e.g., a miniature in Rabula's Book of the Gospels. The iconographic origins, or influences, affecting these works are easily recognisable: the sepulchre is shaped like an Eastern chapel, and like a Western sarcophagus.

Soon afterwards, Peter and John, told by Mary Magdalene of what she had found, go to the sepulchre: this is St. John's record: "Peter therefore went forth, and that other disciple, and came to the sepulchre. So they ran both together: and the other disciple did outrun Peter, and came first to the sepulchre. And he, stooping down, *and looking in*, saw the linen clothes lying; yet went he not in. Then cometh Simon Peter following him, and went into the sepulchre, and seeth the linen clothes lie, And the napkin, that was about his head, not lying with the linen clothes, but wrapped together in a place by itself. Then went in also that other disciple, which came first to the sepulchre, and he saw, and believed." *(John 20 : 3-8.)*

The above text gave rise to an artistic style which, though just as old as that illustrating the women at the sepulchre, is very much less known. It seems to have come to an end at the time of the Renaissance, despite its obvious apologetic value, being the eye-witness account of an apostle, indeed of two apostles.

For about eight centuries, artists seemed very uncertain as to how they should portray the Resurrection, especially how to depict Jesus. Should He be fully dressed, or swathed in the linen clothes? Again, did He Himself roll the stone away from the door of the sepulchre, or did angels help Him? In any event, how was the Resurrection to be made different from the Ascension? An important change took place in about the eleventh century. Realism took the place of symbolism and of the allusiveness of the scene of the women at the sepulchre.

This realism was a great change, which occurred considerably later than the similar change as regards the Crucifixion, and the most probable explanation is that, by representing Christ as actually rising from the tomb, there was being shown also the promise of the resurrection of the faithful who had died in Christ.

Various solutions of these difficult artistic problems were tried. Réau enumerates five principal ones:

1. Christ sits up in His sarcophagus.
2. He puts one foot on its edge.
3. He strides out of the sarcophagus.
4. He stands upright in front of it.
5. He stands upright on the top of it.

In pictures of Christ getting out of the tomb, He is always shown carrying a banner with a Cross on it, symbol of His victory over death. In Germany, the intricate and absurd treatment of this subject often disguised its sacredness. In Italy, Giotto introduced a new way of picturing the Resurrection. Instead of a Christ standing in the tomb, he pictures a Christ floating above it in the air. This naturally got mixed up with the Ascension and the Transfiguration. It remained typically Italian during the fourteenth and fifteenth centuries, but later spread farther afield.

The Counter-Reformation theologians decreed that the risen Christ must be shown either on the tomb or in front of it, that the tomb must be shut, and that His body must show an immaterial radiance and be clothed in a red garment in such a way as to show His wounds.

Having risen when no witnesses were present, Jesus showed Himself first to the holy women, then to the apostles, and finally to about five hundred brethren, thus confirming that He really had risen and giving them confidence to spread the good news.

Regarding the appearances of the risen Lord, the documents differ, but it is not the business of iconography to concern itself with Biblical exegesis. Christian art seeks to satisfy the liturgical and teaching needs of the Church. Our Lord's appearances are usually divided into two groups, those in Jerusalem and those in Galilee. At the end of the Middle Ages, there was a widely-held popular belief—going back to Byzantine sources and influenced by the Golden Legend—that Jesus' first appearance was to Mary, His mother. This is mentioned in none of the Sacred Scriptures, but the belief became so widespread that Ignatius Loyola makes it the subject of a meditation in his famous *Spiritual Exercises*. And Teresa of Avila also thinks that Jesus kept His first visit after His Resurrection for His Mother. In some pictures Jesus appears alone to His Mother; in others He has with Him the Patriarchs of the Old Covenant, whom He introduces to her. This subject was fully illustrated throughout the fifteenth, sixteenth, and seventeenth centuries, especially in the West. It satisfied the feelings of the faithful, who felt rather shocked at the thought that Jesus had appeared first to Mary Magdalene, a sinner, in preference to His own mother. If there be no scriptural basis for Our Lord's appearance to His mother, there is plenty for that to Mary Magdalene: "She (Mary Magdalene) turned herself back, and saw Jesus standing, and knew not that it was Jesus. Jesus saith unto her, Woman, why weepest thou? whom seekst thou? She, supposing him to be the gardener, saith unto him, Sir, if thou have borne him hence, tell me where thou hast laid him, and I will take him away. Jesus saith unto her, Mary. She turned herself, and saith unto him, Rabboni;

which is to say, Master. Jesus saith unto her, Touch me not; for I am not yet ascended to my Father: but go to my brethren, and say unto them, I ascend unto my Father, and your Father; and to my God, and your God." *(John 20 : 14-17.)*

There are also references in Matthew 28 : 9, 10, and Mark 16: 9, and the latter states specifically that "he appeared first to Mary Magdalene."

Though varying in details, the artistic treatment of this theme is very old, being found since the fourth century. Jesus sometimes avoids Mary Magdalene, and sometimes pushes her away by her forehead. Jesus' dress varies with the time: first a toga; then His shroud; and finally He is dressed as a gardener, and in the fourteenth century, He even has on a large hat and holds a spade. Sometimes He holds both a spade and the standard of the Resurrection. For centuries this scene—"Noli me tangere" ("Touch me not") as it was called—was very popular, but nowadays it does not seem to inspire contemporary artists. A very few examples are found in churches in Asia and Africa.

Of Jesus' appearances to the apostles, either together or singly, those most popular with artists are His appearance to the two disciples on the road to Emmaus and His appearance to Thomas and all the apostles.

On the day after the sabbath, two disciples started walking to Emmaus, a village about seven miles from Jerusalem. As they went, Jesus joined them and went with them. He asked them questions and, without making Himself known to them, "beginning with Moses and all the prophets, he expounded unto them in all the scriptures the things concerning Himself." *(Luke 24 : 27.)*

This first part of St. Luke's account is the subject of one of the mosaics in the Church of St. Apollinare Nuovo at Ravenna and is still used by artists. The second part of the Gospel story, the meal at Emmaus, started a fashion that is more recent but much more widespread.

Jesus also appeared twice to His apostles when they were assembled behind locked doors. On the first occasion, Thomas was absent, and when told of the appearance later said he would not believe unless he actually saw and touched Jesus. The second occasion was a week later, when Thomas was present, and Jesus said to him, "Reach hither thy finger, and behold my hands; and reach hither thy hand, and thrust it into my side: and be not faithless, but believing. And Thomas answered and said unto him, My Lord and my God. Jesus saith unto him, Thomas, because thou hast seen me, thou hast believed: blessed are they that have not seen, and yet have believed." *(John 20 : 27-29.)*

The oldest illustrations of this Gospel story date from the fifth century—the sarcophagus in the Ravenna Museum and the British Museum ivory. And, in this century, a Chinese artist of the Peking school has also illustrated it. Its universal popularity with artists stems clearly from the teaching value of the incident, for in the light of the lesson Thomas received, who could persist in doubt?

Jesus had told the apostles that He would go before them into Galilee, where He would meet them. And so the Gospels record some of His post-Resurrection appearances as occurring there: e.g., the great catch of fish, in the added Chapter 21 of the Fourth Gospel. Artists who have illustrated this scene have rightly seen it as a method used by Jesus to impress on His apostles their mission as fishers of men, instead of merely another feeding miracle. Indeed, that is the mission of all Christians, prefigured in this miracle.

This Galilean appearance of Our Lord has been a great deal less illustrated than events that took place there before the Resurrection, in spite of its symbolical value. Indeed, during His incarnate life, Jesus had shown forth His

glory in Galilee. The Gospels mention the stilling of the storm *(Matthew 8 : 26, Mark 4 : 39, Luke 8 : 24)*, Jesus walking on the water on the Lake of Tiberius *(Matthew 14 : 25, Mark 6 : 48, John 6 : 19)*, and also the Transfiguration.

The oldest of these events to be illustrated is Jesus' Walking on the Water, which is the subject of a third-century frieze in the Christian Chapel at Doura-Europos. The Stilling of the Storm was illustrated only three centuries later, being found on the column of a sixth-century canopy in St. Mark's, Venice. Since then, this scene has been constantly illustrated, and the Indian artist, Alfred Thomas, has recently given it an Indian setting.

An interesting detail is the way the setting of the lake scene changes. Conrad Witz's painting of the miraculous draught of fishes is set on the Lake of Geneva: and for the frescoes at Oberzell (Reichenau) the Lake of Constance forms the background.

The Transfiguration occupies a particularly important place in the earthly life of Jesus. This appearing of the Lord in Glory is related in the three Synoptic Gospels, though ignored by St. John, and is alluded to in 2 Peter 1: 16-18. According to St. Augustine and St. Thomas Aquinas, the Transfiguration should be seen as a manifestation of the Holy Trinity: in the midst of a luminous cloud, the symbol of the Holy Spirit, God the Father proclaims Jesus as His well-beloved Son.

In the Eastern Church, the Transfiguration soon became, and still remains, one of the important and popular feasts. In the West, the monks of Cluny encouraged it, and it appears for the first time in Spain in the ninth century. It was made a feast of the whole Church in 1457, and August 6 was fixed as its date.

The artistic representation of this scene was at first accomplished symbolically, as can be seen in the mosaic in the small apse of the Church of St. Apollinare in Classe at Ravenna. A jewelled Cross, enclosed in a circle and standing out against a background of a starry sky, hints at Christ's presence. The head and shoulders of Moses and Elias emerge from clouds, and three lambs take the place of the apostles. This is probably a unique example of a symbolical representation of the Transfiguration.

At about the same period, we have pictures of Christ Transfigured at Constantinople (Church of the Holy Apostles) and at Sinai (Monastery of St. Catherine). The problem of how to make Jesus' face "shine as the sun" and His "raiment white as the light" *(Matthew 17 : 1, 2)* proved a difficult one. In general, artists either surrounded Christ's body with a halo, or used golden yellow paint. This type of artistic work was more frequently done in miniatures and paintings than in sculpture. Today, the Churches of Asia and Africa are starting on this theme, which has been widespread both in the West and in the East, where it began.

The risen Christ's last appearance to the apostles was at His Ascension. This is recorded quite shortly in St. Luke's Gospel 24: 50-52: "And he led them out as far as to Bethany, and he lifted up his hands, and blessed them. And it came to pass, while he blessed them, he was parted from them, and carried up into heaven. And they worshipped him, and returned to Jerusalem with great joy."

So brief a passage does not give much scope for artistic illustration, but the first chapter of The Acts of the Apostles goes into rather more detail: "And when he had spoken these things, while they beheld, he was taken up; and a cloud received him out of their sight. And while they looked steadfastly toward heaven as he went up, behold, two men stood by them in white apparel. Which also said, Ye men of Galilee, why stand ye gazing up into heaven? This same Jesus, which is taken up from you into heaven, shall so come in like manner as ye have seen him go into heaven." *(Acts 1 : 9-11.)*

The two details mentioned in this passage—the cloud that hid Jesus, and the angels foretelling Christ's coming again in judgment—were taken up into the iconography of the Ascension.

The oldest illustration of the Ascension which we have is of Greek origin: a small ivory plaque, now in the Bavarian National Museum. It shows Jesus rising to the skies by climbing up a mountain slope, and God the Father's hand, coming through a cloud, is seen stretching out to Him.

An artistic development is seen in such pieces as the ampulla of Monza (fifth century), Rabula's Book of the Gospels (sixth century) and a coptic fresco at Baouit. In these, the Ascended Christ is already in heaven, either sitting or standing, and surrounded by a halo.

Byzantine art shows Christ in a medallion or aureole. Artists of the Near East, specially conscious of Christ's divinity, represent Him full-face, motionless, and radiating glory: the Ascension became an apotheosis.

In the following centuries, Western art developed its own style, different from that of the East. More conscious of Christ's humanity, they tried to bring out the movement in a scene. In addition, Western style developed and evolved through the centuries, whereas that of the East remained unalterable.

From the eleventh century, Christ ascends without any help, either from His Father, or from specially appointed angels: this accorded with the teaching of the Roman Catholic Church. This latter style allows for many variations. Sometimes Christ's head emerges through a cloud, held like a carpet by two angels (Cloister of Silos, Spain, thirteenth century). Sometimes His feet alone are visible. According to Meyer Schapiro, this last development was due to English influence, which sought to copy the extreme brevity of the Gospel account. A third method was to show Christ whole, in spite of the risk of confusing the Ascension with the Resurrection or the Transfiguration.

At the Renaissance, the religious scene of the Ascension became an excuse for showing a pagan triumphal procession, in imitation of those of ancient Rome. Luckily, the fashion failed to oust the traditional method of representing the Ascension, which has become world-wide, as we see from the many examples produced in the missionary countries.

The Ascension, though it ended the earthly ministry of Jesus, did not become the last subject for portrayal of Christ in Glory. We read in Matthew 24: 30-31: "And then shall appear the sign of the Son of man in heaven: and then shall all the tribes of the earth mourn, and they shall see the Son of man coming in the clouds of heaven with power and great glory. And he shall send his angels with a great sound of a trumpet, and they shall gather together his elect from the four winds, from one end of heaven to the other."

The theme of the Second Coming of Christ gave rise to an important iconography, drawn partly from the Revelation of St. John the Divine and partly from the Gospels.

The prelude to the Last Judgment is the war between Christ and Antichrist, and Christ's victory over Satan. As this episode is described in the Book of Revelation, it will be convenient to begin the last part of this chapter on Christ in Glory by considering some of the scenes in that book. There is no intention to write here an analysis or exegesis of the Book of Revelation, but merely to describe some of the very many portraits of Christ, painted, engraved, and carved, that that book's poetical and prophetic value have inspired. We will give only a few examples. The first theophany is thus described in the first chapter of Revelation: "And in the midst of the seven candlesticks one like unto the Son of man, clothed with a garment down to his foot, and girt about the paps with a golden girdle. His head and his hairs were white like wool, as white as snow; and his eyes were as a flame of fire; and his feet like unto fine brass, as if they burned in a furnace; and his voice as the sound of

many waters. And he had in his right hand seven stars; and out of his mouth went a sharp two edged sword: and his countenance was as the sun shineth in his strength." *(Revelation 1 : 13-16.)*

It proved difficult to translate the above into artistic representations, and artists took considerable liberties with the text. It is illustrated in stained glass windows, in tapestries, engravings, and miniatures, but rarely in statuary after the twelfth century, when the second theophany became more popular.

This second vision is recorded in Chapter 4 of Revelation. Christ (though not actually named) is seated on a throne, surrounded by four and twenty elders wearing crowns of gold on their heads, and by four beasts— a lion, a calf, a man, and an eagle. And before the throne "there was a sea like unto crystal."

This vision, more suitable for artistic representation than the first, is, iconographically, among the most important of medieval times. The tympani at the Church of St. Peter's, Moissac, at St. James, Compostelle, and at the Cathedral at Chartres, are but a few examples among many. However, after the thirteenth century, the Christ of the Apocalypse ceased to be represented in statuary; the Christ of the Last Judgment, based on St. Matthew's Gospel, was becoming more popular.

Chapter 5 of the Revelation gives another vision of Jesus. As no one had been found worthy to open the book sealed with seven seals (symbol of the Divine Revelation), Jesus appeared in the form of a lamb "as it had been slain," and took the book. And the elders and beasts fell down before the lamb and sang His praises. This theme never became as popular as the last one, and the best examples of works illustrating it can be given quickly: the Tapestry of the Apocalypse at Angers, Van Eyck's Mystical Lamb, and Dürer's Apocalypse.

Other pictures derived from the Book of Revelation are: Christ with the sickle, reaping the earth's harvest *(14 : 14)*; and Christ seated on a white horse, called "Faithful and True . . . his eyes were as a flame of fire . . . and he was clothed with a vesture dipped in blood: and his name is called The Word of God." *(19 : 11-13.)*

These vast compositions derive many of their visions from the Book of Revelation, such as Christ with the sharp sword and with the sickle. These scenes must not, however, be confused with those of the Last Judgment itself; the former are multiple and succeed each other, whereas the Last Judgment, inspired by St. Matthew's Gospel, consists (in Eastern churches on the inside, in Western churches on the outside) of lines placed one above the other, which must be read from top to bottom. This arrangement is unique in Christian iconography, and was probably influenced by imperial Rome and Byzantium. Reading from the bottom upwards, one finds: the resurrection of the dead, the weighing of souls, the separation of the elect from the damned, and, at the top of it all, Christ the Judge, "coming in the clouds of heaven with power and great glory." *(Matthew 24: 30.)*

There were in succession three variations in the symbol of Christ as the Final Judge. First, Christ is shown with a sharp sword proceeding from His mouth: this follows the Apocalypse. Secondly, as Christ in Majesty, He rides on "clouds of great glory," His right hand raised in blessing, His left holding the Book. Finally, He is portrayed as He died on the Cross, showing His wounds and with the Virgin Mary and John the Baptist on either side of Him.

The mosaic at Torcello, near Venice, is the most complete example of this scene in Byzantine art: in the West, nearly all the tympani of Gothic churches show a Last Judgment at the main door.

Taken out of its context of the Last Judgment, the portrait of Christ the Judge becomes that of Christ the King. This development occurred to such an extent that all trace of its artistic origins was lost. A "Christ the King," by the African artist Woellfel, makes it clear that many churches today have little or no cultural connection with Europe or the Near East. Christian iconography is in the midst of a revolutionary change: the medieval traditions which still influence the West have no influence on those civilizations which do not share the same historical background. Men picture Christ differently, and find new methods of picturing the scenes of the Holy Scriptures.

Every age has produced portrayals of Christ in Glory. Sometimes these were based solely on the New Testament, sometimes they bore evidence of the religious aspirations of a whole people, and sometimes they reflected only the devotional fashion of a particular group or a particular period. These devotional fashions had varied successes: some just disappeared; some evolved a certain way and then faded out. The present period has few good portraits of Christ in Glory, although such themes as the Transfiguration, the Resurrection, and the Ascension hold so important a place in the Church's teaching that they will always demand illustrations for instruction. But Christian art, with the possible exception of architecture, is in a sorry state, being absorbed in lifeless technicalities or in a too-studied return to the primitive.

And yet no civilization has had so many pictures. The printing press, the cinema and television make their way into every home. These provide our idols, in a world where competition has become a pitiless struggle and international relations have deteriorated into a state of cold war or the threat of annihilation.

But Christians know that God's kingdom is not of this world. They pray that His kingdom may come, and that grace may be given to all, enabling them to develop the Christian virtues, especially the love of God and their neighbours, so that by their lives men may bear witness to Christ. Above all, Christians pray that they may be enabled so to live their faith that the world may again say, as it did in the days of Tertullian (*Apologetical, 39, 7*), "see how they love one another."

CHRIST THE KING – AUSTRIA

These small oil-paintings on glass, produced by the people for the people, may be regarded as the icons of the West. These works, which had their origin in religion and folklore, and which have been prevalent from Poland to Spain since the end of the seventeenth century, have now become collectors' pieces. If their authors sometimes treat the same subjects as the great masters did, it is because both have drawn from the same fountainhead for their inspiration: it is not mere copying by the former. The subjects and styles vary with their places of origin.

In this Christ, shown both as Child and King, we have an example—and there are others in this book—of popular religious art before the invention of colour-printing which, being so much cheaper to produce, threatens with extinction an art in which is reflected the piety and genius of simple folk.

162

Until the eleventh century the Resurrection was depicted allusively or by symbol: an empty tomb guarded by an angel and discovered by the two holy women. This, indeed, illustrated the Gospel text. It was not until the second half of the Middle Ages that the risen Christ Himself was portrayed, a theme which developed until the Renaissance. Christ stands up, sometimes in the tomb, sometimes in front or even on the top of it. He is also shown actually getting out of a sarcophagus.

Christ always carries a standard stamped with a Cross, symbol of His victory over death. Later, under Italian influence, He is painted above the tomb, an innovation which gave a suitable dynamic quality to the iconography of the Resurrection.

164

THE ASCENSION — GERMANY

THE ASCENSION — GOSPEL OF FULDA

THE ASCENSION — USA   THE ASCENSION, BY GEORGE WANG — CHINA

This fourth-century ivory from Munich shows God the Father helping Christ to ascend to the heavens. As from the tenth century, Christ ascends unaided. The two important details of this iconographic theme, viz. the cloud which hides Jesus from His disciples, and the two angels who tell them, "this same Jesus, which is taken up from you into heaven, shall so come in like manner as ye have seen Him go into heaven" are, of course, taken from the Acts of the Apostles.

During the Renaissance, the Ascension became an excuse for triumphal pictures after the Roman fashion, void of any connection with religion. But, anyhow, the traditional theme survived better than the ideas of the six-teenth-century humanists.

168

CHRIST IN GLORY – VATICAN

The fourth chapter of the Book of the Revelation inspires the tympanum of the Church of Moissac, France. Christ is shown in majesty, surrounded by the four beasts; "and the first beast was like a lion, and the second beast was like a calf, and the third beast had the face as a man, and the fourth beast was like a flying eagle." *(Revelation 4:7.)* There is no doubt that these creatures were given a symbolic meaning: according to Saint Gregory they symbolised four attributes of Christ, man by His birth, calf by His death, lion by His resurrection, and eagle by His ascension. However, the exegesis of Saint Irenaeus and Saint Jerome was preferred, according to which the man represents Saint Matthew, because his Gospel opens with the human genealogy of Christ; the lion represents Saint Mark, because in his first verses he writes of "the voice of one crying in the wilderness"; the eagle represents Saint John's effortless soaring to eternal truths; and the calf represents Saint Luke, because his Gospel begins with the story of John the Baptist's father, Zacharias, a priest who offered sacrifice.

CHRIST TRIUMPHANT — GERMANY

Some periods of history have been fortunate in that a happy balance has been struck between the flights of inspired imagination on the one hand, and the refinements of form in their material expression on the other. The Romanesque and Gothic were two such periods.

The Romanesque sculptors light up, as if in lightning flashes, the deepest truths and mysteries of the Faith. Their Christs in Majesty are superhuman heroes. On the other hand, Gothic sculpture brings us back to ourselves, with its greater emphasis in God's love and human frailty. The Gothic Christ is indeed a father who teaches and judges, but always with that loving gentleness which pervades the Gospels.

174

" BEAU-DIEU " – FRANCE

When compared with the Christ on the tympanum of the Church at Moissac, this statue shows the way art developed after the Romanesque period. The almost royal grandeur of this Christ of the Abbey of Saint-Viet seems to have deprived it of all religious feeling. The realism which developed in Christian art deprived it of all sense of the luminous, leaving the observer no time for meditation or prayer.

Pilate asked Jesus, "Art thou a king then?" to which Jesus replied, "Thou sayest that I am a king." So Pilate had fixed to the top of the Cross the inscription "Jesus of Nazareth, King of the Jews". In the monastic Byzantine art Christ is first pictured dressed in imperial or episcopal vestments, signifying that He is the supreme sovereign. A similar inspiration has led the African artist, Woellfel, to paint Christ dressed as one of his native chiefs. One angel holds a sceptre, and another a symbol of great personal importance in Africa, an umbrella, on which are stamped the symbols of faith, hope and charity.

CHRIST THE KING, BY WOELLFEL — AFRICA   CHRIST-BISHOP — GREECE

In view of the widespread observance by Roman Catholics of the devotion to the Sacred Heart of Jesus, its liturgical observance was permitted in 1765, when Pope Clement XIII authorized the Mass and Office of the Feast. Since then the cult has spread to all the corners of the world. As an iconographic subject it has supplanted the Teaching Christ and the Triumphant Christ, the Christ of the Last Judgment. But we know of no work of any merit, religious or artistic; on the contrary, there exist a large number of objects in the worst taste. In the circumstances it is better to consider the anonymous African artist, author of this statue which, though awkward in execution, has dignity and expressiveness.

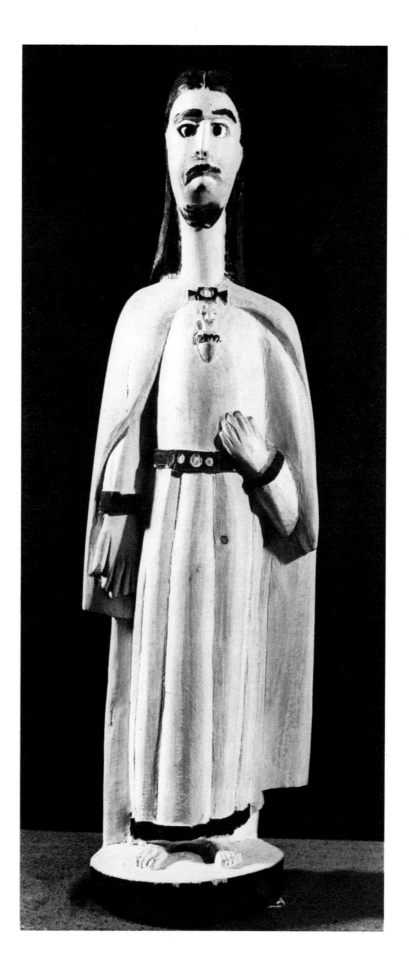

The doctrine of the Holy Trinity was defined and promulged by the Council of Nicaea in A.D.325, and that century has left us one iconographic representation of the doctrine on a sarcophagus in the Lateran Museum. The depicting of the doctrine proved a difficult matter, and certain plastic interpretations were regarded with disfavour. For instance, the Council of Trent condemned the use of a three-headed man to represent the Trinity. The use of the Trinity as an iconographic motif became widespread, especially in catholic countries. This sometimes took a symbolical form, e.g. an equilateral triangle with an eye or a circle in it, but more usually the form was figurative—three people placed either horizontally or vertically or in the shape of a triangle. Very often the Holy Spirit appeared as a dove.

Without entirely breaking away from Western form, the Indian artist Da Fonseca has taken his inspiration from the Vedas, the pre-Christian sacred books of Hinduism. This painting suggests the characteristically Indian idea of a cosmic inspiration, but the presentation is thoroughly Christian.

182

Christian art, inherited from the Middle Ages, from Byzantium and from Rome, today seems played out, effete.

An ancient world crumbles, the rhythms of life are unsettled, tradition ceases to have authority, and spiritual values become corrupted and lost. A new world is being born, selective, dynamic, in a state of flux, and unforgiving.

So this generation must recreate a civilization. Christians must accept the challenge of this turning-point in history and, by seeking to reconcile the old and the new, respond to mankind's desperate need for love and brotherhood—in short, carry out their Master's teaching.

If we all based our lives on Faith, Hope, Love and Justice, we should perform miracles for the good of mankind and the greater glory of God.

Only in this way will our generation be able to hand on to those to come a new Christian art, different in its forms of expression, but inspired by the great unchanging truths of our religion of the divine Son of Man.

APPENDIX

No work under the signature of an established European master appears in this book. These can be found in other works, e.g. "The Life of Christ in Masterpieces of Art and the Words of the New Testament," Harper & Brothers, New York, 1957; "The Life of Christ," Collins, London, 1959.

Our purpose is different, namely to bring before the reader works which are either unknown or little known, especially of the more popular forms, and also the indigenous Christian art of the missionary countries, showing how these works, of very varying techniques and differing styles, all derive from one common source of inspiration. The pictures have been chosen for their historical and symbolical interest, as well as for their beauty and striking characteristics. The selection is far from exhaustive, and the reader who wishes to pursue his enquiries further may find some helpful suggestions in the pages which follow.

CATALOGUES OF CHRISTIAN ART

There exist two important ones: one at Princeton, U.S.A., and the Vatican; the other at Assisi, Italy.

INDEX OF CHRISTIAN ART
Princeton University, U.S.A.

This indexes some tens of thousands of cards divided into two sections. The first division is by subjects and technical styles. Each card, besides describing the work, gives particulars of where it can be seen, and all biographical references. The second section consists of photographic reproductions, classified according to techniques and countries of origin, which help speedy identification of the motif and state of preservation.

A photostat copy of this enormous catalogue is in the Vatican: both the original and this copy are in constant use. The catalogue includes all Christian works of art from the beginnings of Christianity until the end of the Middle Ages.

PRO CIVITATE CRISTIANA
Assisi, Italy

This is a modern centre of christological study, but it owns an important iconographic catalogue, containing 45,000 photographs. It is of special interest to those concerned with native Christian art and with the works of contemporary artists generally. The centre also owns some original works of Asiatic and African origin, and there is a library, a cinematograph section, and a section devoted to the study of the history of music. All these create this "watch tower" of Christianity.

MUSEUMS AND MISSIONARY BODIES

The various missionary bodies—Catholic and Protestant—have records dealing with Christian art in the different missionary countries. The following is a list, albeit incomplete, of some of these:

GERMANY

The "Zentrale des Papstlichen Werkes der Glaubensverbreitung," in Aachen, has some interesting records and is a real source for bibliographical research.

ENGLAND

The following missionary organisations will provide the seeker with every kind of information, or with photographs, books, addresses, etc.:

Church Missionary Society
6 Salisbury Square
London, E.C. 4

Society for Promoting Christian Knowledge
Holy Trinity Church
Marylebone
London, N.W. 1

Society for the Propagation of the Gospel
15 Tufton Street
London, S.W. 1

FRANCE

Two missionary museums are worth visiting:

Musée des Missions Africaines de Lyon
150, Cours Gambetta
Lyon

Musée de l'Œuvre de la Propagation de la Foi
12, rue Sala
Lyon

ITALY

The missionary Museum of the Lateran, Rome, shows some indigenous works of Christian art but, generally speaking, its interest is mainly ethnological.

N.B. — Different bodies have collected pictures from very many different countries which have often been shown at conferences and exhibitions. Information can be obtained from the following:

The Art Gallery and Museum
Glasgow, C. 3

National Bible Society of Scotland
5, St. Andrew's Square
Edinburgh

The Bible Societies in Malaya
7, Armenian Street
Singapore 6

MUSEUMS AND PUBLIC COLLECTIONS

The large museums exhibit their recognized masterpieces, but many examples of Christian art, often of greater interest, are to be found in local or episcopal museums, and in churches. We cannot, within the compass of these few pages, give particulars; we can but say that the specialised catalogues of these bodies provide valuable works of reference.

CHRISTIAN ART

The general works and monographs on the history of art give those places—museums, churches, etc.—that merit a visit. Of special importance are the works of Kunstle and de Réau (see below).

CHRISTIAN POPULAR ART

It is a great pity that the museums of popular art are so little known, as they often contain important and valuable works—small oil-paintings on glass, engravings, sculptures, etc. The Musées des Arts et Traditions Populaires of Basle, Paris and Rome, have allowed us the fullest access to their treasures. That at Basle is especially well-off in objects of popular Christian art from every part of Europe. There is also an extremely interesting collection in the Musée de l'Imagerie, Epinal.
In the United States of America, the *Index of American Design* contains an enormous collection of 15,000 drawings and watercolours, and 5,000 photographs, among which are examples of Christian art produced in all parts of that country.

The following addresses will prove useful:

Museum of English Rural Life
The University
Shinfield Road
Reading

Inventaire des Œuvres d'Art
Quebec

Musée des Arts et Traditions Populaires
Palais de Chaillot
Paris

Musée de l'Imagerie
Epinal (France)

Musée des Arts et Traditions Populaires
Rome

Musée Ethnographique et Musée Suisse de Folklore
Augustinergasse 2
Basle

Index of American Design
National Gallery of Art
Washington 25, D.C.

GENERAL BIBLIOGRAPHY

It is impossible to give a complete bibliography of so vast a subject: all that can be done is to give what the reader may treat as starting-points.

Basic Works

Réau, Louis
"Iconographie de l'Art Chrétien"
PUF, 1957
T. I   Introduction générale
T. II   Iconographie de la Bible
        (1) Ancien Testament
        (2) Nouveau Testament
T. III Iconographie des Saints — Répertoire — Tables

Kunstle, Karl
"Ikonographie der christlichen Kunst"
Freiburg i. Br. 1928

These two works have important bibliographies which will greatly help the student in his own researches.

At present, there does not exist any one book on the history of art that deals with Christian art, popular art, and indigenous art. As regards the popular arts, no book deals specifically with the Christian popular arts, but the undermentioned will prove useful:

Geiger, P. and Wildhaber, Robert
"Bibliographie des Arts et Traditions Populaires"
Basle

For the arts in missionary countries the following are recommended:

Didinger, Johannes and Streit, Robert
"Bibliotheca Missionum"
Internationales Institut für Missionswissenschaftliche Forschung, Aachen

Didinger G. and Rommerskirchen
"Bibliografia Missionaria"
Rome, 1939

COLOURED PLATES

ACKNOWLEDGEMENTS ARE DUE TO THE FOLLOWING FOR THE SUPPLY OF BLACK AND WHITE PHOTOGRAPHS:

Alinari 134, 175
Appetiti 44, 46, 51, 52, 53, 55, 59, 61-78, 81, 85, 92, 95, 117,
  120-121, 125, 137, 138, 139, 140, 169, 178, 181, 183
Archivio fotografico, Vaticano 96, 170
Archives photographiques, Paris 91, 93, 100
Archivio MAS, Barcelona 45, 144, 145
Blin 54, 77
British Museum 130
Dräyer 119
Ecole Pratique des Hautes Etudes 133
German National Museum, Nuremberg 90
Jeiter 48
Moltzer 122
Missi-Photo 126

Musée des Missions Africaines, Lyon 129
Musée Historique, Basle 165
Musée St. Raymond, Toulouse 47
National Gallery of Art, Washington 168
National Museum of Bavaria 166
National Swiss Museum, Zürich 43, 60, 143, 146, 147, 148
Nationalmuseet, Copenhagen 138
Ohmayer 104, 105
O.P.P., Quebec 103
Pro Civitate Cristiana, Assisi 89
Retzlaff 167, 174, 176
Roubier 82
S.P.G., London 55, 75
Viollet 173

CONTENTS

PRINTED IN SWITZERLAND
by
IMPRIMERIE CENTRALE LAUSANNE

ILLUSTRATIONS ENGRAVED AND PRINTED
by
HÉLIOGRAVURE CENTRALE LAUSANNE